MW01536543

Progressively Restoring
American Greatness

Progressively Restoring American Greatness

By Anthony Watson

ISBN 978-1-257-02092-8

Acknowledgements

To the many people that have engaged me in debate over these issues from the right and left. A special thanks to those that actually took me seriously and engaged in those debates with earnest.

About the Author

Anthony Watson is a native-born Californian, who lives with his wife and two sons behind the Orange Curtain.

Table of Contents

Introduction

The Progressive Double Entendre

On the political right, to be termed a progressive is to be called a dirty word. For a right-winger to support anything progressive is to be called a radical, a hippie, a socialist, a communist, or worse... a Democrat and a liberal, by their fellows. Few on the right seem to remember that Republicans often have been the forerunners of progressive thought in American political history and once proudly claimed the label. It was the so-called Radical Republicans of the middle 19th century that helped bring an end to slavery in America. At the turn of the last century, a progressive movement spearheaded by the conservative Republican Teddy Roosevelt altered the direction of America in the 20th century. That earlier progressive movement at the beginning of the 20th century empowered every American to be all that they could be. At the beginning of the 21st century, our country needs a unifying and empowering political agenda that bridges the current political chasms to restore American greatness.

Progressive also literally means making progress. The implicit positive meaning is that the progress will generally require a certain perseverance and focus to gradually achieve a goal over time. That is the literal meaning of progressive, to make progress. Progressively is a concept that Americans will have to keep in mind, because things are going to get progressively better or they are going to get progressively worse. The status quo cannot stand. Change is in the air.

Americans have dug a big hole financially, and it is going to take a long time to dig out. The depth of our debt is staggering. Paying it down will be a progressive process. We will have to make serious changes throughout our society to begin the long, slow climb out of the mess where America finds itself. Progressively restoring American greatness will require a clear long-term plan executed over decades. All honest Republican and

Democrats will admit that the aforementioned statements are true, but that is about all they can agree on! This progressive agenda is a long-term plan for gradually restoring American leadership in the world. This book seeks to restore progressively the greatness of our country through consensus.

Unfortunately, to be progressive today is to be deemed a liberal, persona non grata, by half this nation. For the other half, to be progressive is to be a rabble-rouser that gets in the way of Democratic political gain. Most Democrats are frustrated with progressives, and the feeling is mutual. Perhaps a Progressive is not really a Democrat. As a nation, the politics of left and right have prevented "progress" for far too long, and forward progress is clearly a necessity for the 21st century

The Liberal/Conservative chasm that divides us, mirroring the Democrat/Republican fault line, has fractured our nation. Progressive politics laid the groundwork for American ascendancy in the 20th century, and it can do so again. Progressive has certain political connotations today that tend to make many Americans think of unrestrained liberal government…at least in the eyes of most Republicans and right-wing conservatives. It is a sad truth that today's GOP has forgotten that a conservative Republican president, Teddy Roosevelt, shepherded the progressive vision into American politics. Perhaps it irks them that his liberal Democratic cousin, President Franklin Roosevelt then nurtured it.

The current war between the parties has hamstrung us, and so it seemed appropriate to embrace the political title of progressive. It is a title that has history and connections on both sides of the aisle. Progressives should be promoting a forward-thinking political and social agenda for the new challenges we face as a nation and not getting bogged down in partisanship.

This book is meant to appeal to all red-blooded, patriotic Americans, whether they identify themselves as Democrat, Republican, 3rd party, independent, or apolitical. Progressives are not a bunch of lefty ideologues, and progressives are not the left wing of the Democratic Party. A true progressive is a serious person seeking serious solutions to help America and her people progress into the future regardless of party agendas.

This book seeks to knit together a progressive agenda that appeals to concerned Americans and builds a majority that can lead. Make no mistake because this agenda seeks to unite Americans, it requires Americans of every stripe to compromise. Americans must find a common ground, and this book seeks to reveal the common ground that is being concealed by the "fog of partisan war". Whether you call yourself a conservative, a liberal, a Democrat, a Republican, or are unaffiliated, you will find something in this book that you will have a hard time liking. Honestly, I set out to write a book that could unite average Americans and that meant compromises for me as well. I compromised, because united we stand, divided we fall is as true as it ever was. These ideas can allow us to progress together into our future.

Common Sense

Within these pages, I am trying to sketch out, in admittedly broad strokes, a picture of a positive American future. This is a vision that, if forced upon the politicians, will allow America to make progress on her finances and her honor, both of which have been damaged severely at the beginning of this new century. The following progressive ideas are deeply interconnected and can, if executed in concert, truly bring about the American Renaissance that we all crave. This agenda is based upon common sense, not any true genius or inspiration. Included in the common sense I'll admit to a healthy dose of tolerance. Politics and the media in America have polarized society so much that common sense no longer seems to exist. The partisan ideologies pushing common sense to the fringe are driven by moneyed power's desire to protect its elite status and lifestyle.

Freedom and liberty cannot exist in a climate of excessive government and corporate power. We are on the road toward an authoritarian capitalism that minimizes individual liberty. Progressives must seek to promote the freedom that was the original vision of our Founding Fathers. There are a number of obstacles to accomplishing this return to greatness. Without digging our way out of debt, we cannot make the investments in our infrastructure and our people that are essential for restoring our greatness as a nation. Moneyed power has achieved levels of wealth sufficient to build and maintain a private infrastructure, which stifles public infrastructure improvement. Also, the future cannot be bright when we are beholden to so many for our energy needs.

A clear and objective view of the American economy will be required for success. The economic power of the military-industrial complex (and now the terror-industrial complex as well) is based upon conflict. With so much American economic activity related to the defense industry, it destroys our credibility as a peace-loving people, and it sows the seeds of endless conflict and war across the planet...not to mention bankrupting our nation. This agenda attempts to create a synergy of solutions to bring about progress on all the aforementioned fronts.

Politicians have stoked the fires of discord along the left/right axis. The angry, name-calling politics that dominate the airwaves are very destructive to the country. The partisan wars prevent even the discussion of controversial ideas, let alone any real action. The two parties have divided the great issues of the day, without necessarily any rational reasons, other than the other people are on one side. This knee jerk reaction for conservatives to oppose whatever liberals support, and vice versa, leads to little reasoned debate.

Once there were "liberal" Republicans, but those handful that still exist are now known as RINOs, "Republicans in Name Only" by their own party. The two parties have become exclusionary, costing us the special synergy between liberal Republicans and conservative Democrats that once brought about dynamic thinking in our politics. This push and pull tension in four directions instead of two has been lost. The progressive agenda in the following pages could be seen as a libertarian-socialist vision of American politics that seeks to reignite our natural synergies by creating the multi-polar political tension that once made American politics great. To some a libertarian-socialist is a contradiction, a fiction, but I submit that there is an overlapping agenda between all ideologies, if we act as Americans first rather than as ideologues.

The caricature of Uncle Sam on the cover shows how the left/right war cripples us. Uncle Sam has eye patches on both eyes. The one on his right eye is Liberalism, which means this ideology blinds Sam to ideas from the right. The eye patch on his left eye is Conservatism, meaning this ideology refuses to see ideas from the left. Democrats and Republicans are beholden to the polarization of left vs. right and conservative vs. liberal. Each side has so demonized the other that any issue one side picks up, the other must be immediately against. Unfortunately, this leaves poor, old Uncle Sam blind. Americans must throw off the blinders of these *isms* and look objectively for solutions to our society's ills.

We have no shortage of ills! Oh, yes, we have many, many problems today, which presumably the readers are aware of and care about or else they would not have opened this book. Partisan warfare has become so heated that tension between left and right prevent us from finding the solutions that are actually there under our noses.

A bipolar political system under stress can settle into a back and forth swing that never actually makes progress but falls into an illusion of change through ever more drastic swings of the political opinion pendulum. Dramatic swings of political opinion can be revelatory in a multi-polar political universe. However, in the bipolar universe we are just going back and forth from the left to the right and back again, which goes nowhere. Society can have a very short memory. First liberal ideas are all the rage and then conservative, but in the beginning of our republic, there was a clear belief in liberty as the guiding ideology.

That belief in freedom brought us together as one nation and one people and dampened the swing of the pendulum, because freedom cannot help but create a multi-polar, diverse political climate. The Founding Fathers provided us a framework from which to progress, adapt, and evolve over the years, not burdened by divisive, preconceived notions of ideology. Then, the guiding vision was that the individual's freedom and liberty comes before the needs of the State. The focus truly was on the individual and their freedom and not what was best for the State, for business, or the oft cited by anti-constitutionalists, public safety.

No doubt, things have changed a lot since the 18th century, but they have not changed as much as the politicians and ideologues would have us believe. The Constitution and the Bill of Rights are still our best weapons. Like the wielding of any weapon though, it requires courage. It requires the courage to embrace and demand the rights that individuals are guaranteed by our Constitution. Unfortunately, individuals have been tempted to turn over too much of their freedoms to authorities under the influence of the siren song of safety. The Bill of Rights empowers the individual citizen to effect change, but citizens must act and be engaged. Freedom and individual rights are the real defense against those that would loot our nation's treasury and run our country into a ditch.

An interesting thing about history is how often the same pressing problems seem to recur as a particular nation or society matures, grows, and eventually, passes into oblivion. Each ideology or ism of its day attacks these recurring problems—substance abuse, feeding the poor, ensuring civil rights, educating our children, etc—with a very narrow mindset. History has also shown that as the pendulum swings back and forth over time, the swings become ever more violent in each direction. Eventually, the society tears itself apart. The great American social experiment can evolve beyond this rollercoaster ride to civil strife.

Remember, moneyed power and their agents are terrified of the power of the people. The colossal partisan divide and the rabid rhetoric from the right and left are bought and paid for by moneyed power. They will fill the airwaves with more and more docu-dramas of fear to divide us. Through all the wrath and hateful speech, the money moves the wheels of the state behind the scenes. The laws created strip the individual of his rights and ability to prevent moneyed power from getting the legislation they have paid for.

That is what politics in America is really all about today: money and power. When the power of the individual is constrained, the power of money and the state become unrestrained. Unholy alliances between billion dollar corporations and millionaire government officials become ever more self-serving. Political rhetoric is used to fire the partisan furnaces any time the regular guy might actually get some real legislative support.

The healthcare legislation, known as ObamaCare, is a perfect example of partisanship being used as obstruction. Rallies and slogans to defeat the legislation were truly divorced from the realities of the bill, because in partisanship only passion matters, not reason. Privately funded "grassroots" rallies, where misguided Americans shout slogans against socialism and declaring any government healthcare insurance will be incompetent, while at the same time protesting potential cuts to their Medicare and Social Security Benefits, make no sense. To citizens of developed nations on the outside, looking in, the passionate slogans shouted by American citizens about the "Coming Socialist Horror", defy common sense. It is clear to the citizens of most developed nations that there should be a social safety net that governments provide for their citizens.

When common sense is on the fringe, we are in real trouble. The next chapter is meant to establish just how far common sense has been pushed from the middle ground. On September 11, 2001, supposedly, the world changed forever. Perhaps, it did change, but I am unable to understand the complete transformation of our national zeitgeist. American reaction to that event boggled me. We seemed consumed by hate, paranoia, and hell bent for revenge. We let our emotions divorce reason from our national thought processes.

My reactions were on the fringe. How I reacted and how I felt about the attacks on the World Trade Center were considered naïve and foolish by friends and colleagues. I was vilified. I held my head in my hands many a day and wondered when the lunacy and fear mongering would end. I often despaired that the WTC attacks would lead to war that would never end.

Today, I feel a new wave in society. We are beginning to see the mess we are in. There is a willingness to embrace some new ideas in the air. The ideas in this book will first start with empowering individual Americans in their own lives, and most importantly, in their political lives. Moneyed power is not going to give up its money or its power voluntarily, and currently, our laws and legislation are very protective of that power and money.

Empowering individuals can lead to dangerous mob rule without a clear unifying vision of what the society of individuals is hoping to achieve, so this book attempts to survey the undiscovered country of common interests. Staking out today's unknown middle ground will require some compromises by all sides. A new day dawns in the American body politic where tolerance and an eye toward practical solutions for our children's futures will rule the day.

Either we have the courage to be free, or we will not be free. It is so very simple. On 09/11/2001, we proved to the whole world that Americans did have the courage to be free, and then, each day afterward, we seemed to run from that courageous truth that caused the whole world to rally to our side. The moneyed and powerful were terrified by what happened on 9/11, because it stripped away all the theater of the military-industrial complex and showed that only freedom and individual liberty could effectively combat our enemies.

Power to the People

How Freedom and Individual Liberty Stopped the Terrorists

The ideas of freedom and individual liberty have never been more under assault than they are today. The Founding Fathers laid the groundwork for a society so forward thinking and revolutionary that moneyed power had a hard time accepting it, even back then. Within a few generations, the Founding Fathers' ideas and framework were under assault by those elected into power after George Washington. These elected positions of power, in concert with wealthy private citizens and corporate entities, have ever since constantly sought to curtail these rights. Lack of technology severely crippled their efforts to rein in freedom. Until the late twentieth century, the vastness of the country limited meaningful surveillance. Once technology began to offer real intelligence at a national and global scale, there was still substantial resistance to domestic spying by our own government, especially from conservative Republicans.

That changed on September 11, 2001. Now that the fear and suspicion of terrorism has transformed America, those technological abilities are being turned to the curtailment of individual freedom and liberty in the name of safety. Despite Ben Franklin's grim statement of reality, "Those who would give up essential liberty to purchase a little temporary safety deserve neither liberty nor safety", we have done just that. Today Americans are afraid and believe that the sacrifice of some liberty and freedom will make them safer. They are very wrong.

The curtailment of individual liberty and freedom can only make us less safe. This seems counter-intuitive, but it is true. The events of September 11, 2001, clearly illustrate this truth. The cold, harsh reality of that truth is scary and makes us want to hand it off to big government. Unfortunately, big government cannot handle the responsibility—not in its current incarnation, and certainly not without instituting laws and procedures that would seem totalitarian even to our post-9/11 eyes. On September 11, 2001, the government's inherent inability to protect us from this type of attack was clearly demonstrated.

Big government not only failed to uncover the plot, it failed to stop the first plane from hitting its target, and in fact, it failed to stop three out of the four airplanes hijacked on September 11, 2001. The brave people on board stopped Flight 93. They were free people, acting on information available in a free society; they were the ones to stop the only plane that did not hit its target.

This is not meant to condemn the government and the military for failing to stop the other three planes. It is the nature of the bloated bureaucratic beast that is government to react slowly. Government is too big and pondering to react to the increasingly fluid and flexible attacks of 21st century terrorist organizations. Only, we as a people can compete with those organizations. In the years since 09/11/2001, we have given away more and more of our ability to defend ourselves against terrorists. Every time we cede an individual right or liberty, we make ourselves less safe, not more.

Today, the people on board Flight 93 would not be able to stop the terrorists. Today, all communications are subject to snooping due to the Patriot Act. Some DHS flunky would now cut off the cell phone calls that allowed those people on board Flight 93 to come to an enlightened decision as to what action to take. Perhaps, the passengers on Flight 93 fashioned weapons from pocketknives and nail clippers, which would now be denied them.

Even after the 9/11 disasters prompted greater security at airports, passengers stopped the next terrorist attempt aboard an airline. The shoe bomber of 2003, Richard Reid, made it through security and was going to do his dirty deed on board, but he was noticed and restrained by passengers. Passengers stopped the Northwest Airlines bomber of Christmas 2009 as well. These passengers, who ignored seat belt signs and other restraints on their freedom within the cabin, stopped another potential act of airplane terror over eight years after the WTC attacks. Big government failed again, and the answer government provides is always to further restrain passengers and eliminate individual rights.

We are spending a lot of money and setting many bad precedents with these "no constitutional rights" zones being created in our nation's airports. The fear of giving up one's rights makes many want to stay away from airports, but the pressures of business force a different action. Air travel is essential in today's world, so many reluctantly comply. Without clear alternatives, the reluctant comply fatalistically. This fatalism is not justified.

There is an alternative course of action that does a better job of protecting us from terrorists, while still protecting individual freedom and liberty. It is individual freedom and liberty that make us stronger and harder to attack. Conversely, we are actually weaker and easier to attack when we are not protected by the flexibility of freedom. We should roll back much of the body scanning and random searching of individuals, driven by shadowy, computerized databases. A secret no-fly list is simply not very effective when it contains the names of so many innocents. America is free, and its people must have freedom of movement without being required to show their papers. This is what it means to live in a free society.

If America's solution to the terrorist threat is to end the free society we live in, then the terrorists have won! One of the positive effects of America's old style freedoms was the incredible ease that our citizens could move about. A salesperson could hop on a plane at a moment's notice and save that important account, for example. There is an ignored, and difficult to quantify, but very real, economic cost to these burdens that the new security regimen has brought. This drag on our economy has been completely ignored for the last decade.

Reducing this security burden should free up many millions of dollars to be spent more effectively. Specifically, we should have more air marshals. We should harden all the cockpit doors and allow pilots to carry side arms. If we had done nothing more than the aforementioned, we would have prevented repetitions of the World Trade Center bombings. There is no need to repeal the Bill of Rights within airline terminals. The fact is the terrorists are not likely to strike the same place, the same way, so where do we repeal the Bill of Rights next? Everything in our large, mobile society is a potential weapon to be used against us, and we seem on course to eventually expand the "No Bill of Rights" zones to every corner of the nation.

The passengers on Flight 93 showed us the way. They demonstrated the power of the people. The greatness in America lies in her people and the diversity of those people. Due to the history of individual freedom and liberty, one hundred people plucked from the streets and put into an airplane will contain a wide range of people and skills. This is our strength. Among those passengers, may be current and former military personnel, police and firefighters, nurses and doctors, and even some gangbangers, bikers, and an assortment of bad asses, malcontents, and ne'er do wells, but they are all Americans—as messy as that is to live in. If we had done nothing to reform airport security after 9/11, there would have been no recurrence of 9/11, because the passengers on Flight 93 demonstrated the true mettle of Americans.

The phrase, "Let's Roll!" should be immortalized in the American pantheon. Those passengers personified America in their final acts of courage. These civilians, these common Americans, were thrown together by random chance, but they did this nation proud when they stopped that plane. They truly saved lives by sacrificing their own. They made terrorists realize that Americans were not the sheep that we are often portrayed as.

It is the consideration of what happened on Flight 93 that we find the most confidence that our Founding Fathers' elevation of the rights of the individual above all else, truly is the correct course. Not only is this the correct course, but a more defensible course than ever before. It is what makes America such a complicated, trailblazing experiment in human culture. We need to take back our country from the fear-mongers and take charge of our own safety and security again.

This book's overriding theme is about America's citizens standing up and setting the agenda for the politicians. Years after September 11, 2001, the course we took as a nation was obviously wrong. We allowed the politicians, liberal and conservative, to tell us what was best for us, rather than recognizing that the passengers of Flight 93 had shown us the way. The people of this nation must step up and take control of the ship of state by exercising their rights as free American citizens.

Let the politicians work out the details, but the leadership must come from us. Freedom is not free. We must think and understand the issues. We must question authorities that seek to retain power for themselves. Of course, America's citizens cannot take the power back if we are too afraid. Politicians will always feed our fears to preserve their power and take the path of least resistance to stay in office. Unless we stand up and take responsibility for our nation and her policies, the government of the people, by the people, and for the people shall perish from this Earth.

Jury Nullification

Jury nullification is the lost check of the people against government overreaching. America's Constitution was meant to create a system of checks and balances that would prevent tyranny. The Founding Fathers meant to make sure that our government had to go to twelve citizens every time they intended to rob another citizen of property or freedom. This has long been a controversial topic in America. The Establishment has dealt with those who speak of jury nullification by throwing them in jail for contempt of court. It is difficult to swim upstream on this, unless the people and the media speak out in favor it. Again, this is another scary idea of our founders, because it puts the power to interpret the law into the hands of the 12 men and women on the jury. The 12 people on the jury are supposed to be able to vote their conscience and decide for themselves whether the law applies or the law is just.

One of the keystones of a new progressive agenda must be citizen empowerment. America's future rests upon whether or not individual citizens will step up and shoulder the burdens of citizenship. As we give more and more power to the government, we must realize that we are really giving power to the wealthy and big business lobbies. Power to the People will require an incredible amount of tolerance from each one of us, because freedom is a messy business. We will need to tolerate many differing opinions, lifestyles, and religious beliefs to forge a coalition large enough to overwhelm the moneyed power that has a chokehold on our government.

Jury nullification opponents will scream anarchy and point to trials in the South that let Ku Klux Klan members go free for lynching that everyone knew they had committed. However, the Constitution clearly gives the central government the power to protect individual rights when states and local lawmakers attempt to abridge citizen rights. Cries from the law-and-order crowd of anarchy and chaos always target the citizenry's most fearful visions, which saturate the media in the numerous flavors of cop shows and endless news cycles of gruesome crimes drawn from all across the country. We must trust our fellow citizens. Anarchy would not result, because an overwhelming majority of Americans want the bad guys to go to jail and will put them there.

The whole idea behind the American jury system was that we might allow 99 guilty men to go free before imprisoning one innocent man. If we do not embrace that most basic concept of our nation's founding, we cannot return to greatness. The Founding Fathers and the Constitution created a justice system that might let 99 guilty individuals go free before imprisoning one innocent, because that system was a huge check on government power. Police can arrest people all day, but if they cannot convict them through constitutional means, their power is checked. The power of the central government to impose its will upon the people was limited as well by this system. Jury nullification is the ultimate check on government power.

The power of jury nullifications means that government cannot pass laws that less than 95% of the people agree with. How do we come to this calculation? Simple, given the requirement of a jury of 12 peers agreeing unanimously to provide a guilty verdict, we divide 1 by 12, which allows for an 8% disagreement percentage. This leads to a 92% agreement threshold in the populace for successful implementation of a given law. However, the ability for a citizen to get at least one appeal on any conviction raises the bar. This guaranteed appeal cuts the 8% threshold to a 4% disagreement threshold among regular citizens being sufficient to influence the central government's ability to prosecute a given law. That means that 96% of the populace must agree with a law to send an individual to jail. What a check on government power to imprison its own populace! With the requirement of 96% agreement, how could America have become the largest imprisoner of its own citizens? America has an enormous prison population and imprisons more of its citizenry than any other "civilized" nation by raw numbers and by per capita. This is freedom? No! It is not freedom. We should all live in great fear of the growing police power of our central government.

Only jury nullification can stop this horrible abuse of the central government's power to make law. Years ago, when George Bush, Sr. went into Panama and dragged Manuel Noriega back to the U.S. for a trial, many questioned the legitimacy of such a military action (but that is for another essay). Our own international legal experts deemed the military intervention legal, of course. Nonetheless, at the trial, the American people spoke out in the courtroom. The people questioned the legitimacy of Bush the First's kidnapping of a foreign leader. In the end, the reality was that the government could not get a conviction. To George Bush, Sr.'s great dismay, there was a hung jury.

The jurors could not agree that Noriega deserved to be imprisoned for the alleged drug trafficking that he was charged with. Many citizens questioned our interpretation of international law that allowed us to invade Panama as well as using the military to pursue and capture a foreign head of state. America's own system of justice could not and would not convict Noriega. Apparently, not only was it a violation of international law as foreign international legal experts had claimed, but it was also a violation of American law, according to America's own citizen jury.

Well, of course, the administration could not stand for an outcome like that. Bush, Sr. had mobilized the military to invade a sovereign nation, captured the duly elected leader of that country, and brought him back to the United States. There had been much international protest over this Christmas invasion. Many protestors referenced Noriega's previous high standing with our government as an ally in the Drug War. Noriega seemed to be receiving punishment for some transgression in his dealings with the CIA, and this was the contention of many within, and without, the U.S. borders. What an embarrassment it would have been for Bush if Noriega had not been imprisoned!

Therefore, the jury was marched before a group of government operatives and presented with "secret evidence". What was the secret evidence that never saw the light of day? We still do not know. We may never know. Perhaps the government officials simply told the jury that they either convict Noriega or go to jail themselves. This is an obviously strong motivation to ignore one's conscience and save one's skin. And so, Noriega went to jail, but it was far from a legal trial. After all, it was obviously a case of jury tampering, which is a federal offense, but by then, the government had already largely exempted itself from such mundane constraints as the Constitution and the rule of law.

If one needs more convincing that the loss of "Jury Nullification" has broken the American justice system, one only need look at the Rodney King beating and the subsequent trial of the officers involved. Many were dismayed by the acquittal of those officers. The evidence was right there on videotape of what was done to Rodney King. No one is saying that Rodney King is a pillar of virtue, but even if he were on PCP, which is arguable, the tape showed him on the ground and cuffed with multiple officers continuing to deliver blows to an obviously helpless individual. How can that not be police brutality?

The jury is not to blame here. The Founding Fathers saw the judge as an impartial arbiter of facts and fairness in the courtroom, not an ally of the prosecution. Unfortunately, in 21st century America the judge does as act as an ally to the prosecution. The jury received strict instructions from the judge that they could not convict the officers if the Los Angeles Police Department had trained them to beat Rodney King in this manner. Huh? Surely, jurors were confused by these instructions, and maybe they even wished to vote their conscience, despite those instructions. Unfortunately, they were faced with a jail term if they were to vote any other way, because of the judge's unconstitutional powers to imprison them for voting their conscience. Contempt of court has been used as a club to beat juries into submission for decades now.

Following the police officers' acquittal, there were riots that on the surface had a racial component. Nonetheless, much of what happened on the day of the acquittal was an assertion of power by the people. It was more than the black versus white rioting that the media and government portrayed it as. Many people hit the streets to protest the acquittal. Some of the rioting may have been a subconscious desire to send a message to the Establishment that though they owned the courtroom and made the laws, the streets were still owned by the people in those South L.A. neighborhoods.

Following this disastrous ruling, the Clinton administration came in and retried the case, further demonstrating the broken state of the American justice system by violating constitutional protections against double jeopardy. The central government got around this with the torturous logic of claiming that the officers had violated Rodney King's civil rights. Despite the ultimate outcome, the retrial only made the whole situation worse by failing to address the strict jury instructions that judges have been allowed to force upon helpless jurors.

The true intent of the jury system is for there to be a constant vote of the people on the laws being put out from the government. To accomplish this, we must fund jury service. There is no way a hard-working stiff can get a jury of his peers. All his peers are hard-working stiffs too. All the accused's true peers are working for companies that do not pay for any jury service. This must change. The federal government must fund this essential part of the American justice system. Verified by pay stubs and/or tax returns, jury compensation should be a more reasonable recompense for this essential citizen service than what is currently being done. The society must fund the salary of people called to jury service for our justice system to work correctly.

Is this too expensive? How much are we willing to pay for freedom? Rolling back the police state would likely reduce costs considerably. Repeatedly, progressives must push the theme of Power to the People. Yes, the people are the great unwashed of our nation in the eyes of many. Together the people, the poor, the blue collar, the middle-class, all outnumber the moneyed, the powerful, the wealthy titans of business, and that is why those same titans are constantly beating the drums of fear among the middle class. The moneyed and powerful will go to their default propaganda that criminals will take over, rape our daughters, and kill our sons. This is the constant drumbeat of television shows like "CSI this" and "CSI that" or "Law and Order this" and "Law and Order that". It will only be a brave and tolerant citizenry that will be able to resist this drumbeat.

Protecting Privacy

Expectations of privacy in the modern era have been eroded beyond all recognition to the 20th-century eye. Our radical freedom-loving precursors of the 18th century would be truly appalled at the government intrusion into individual privacy. For centuries, the expectations of privacy were quite high, even in public spaces. In the last decade or two, spurred by moneyed power and law enforcement do-gooders, such expectations of a private life have been scaled back. By the time that the planes ran into the towers in 2001, privacy had already suffered serious abridgement. However, the 9/11 terrorist attacks sent the last vestiges of privacy out the window, and fear drove a massive expansion of police powers in this country. Driven by fear, most Americans were happy to be searched at the airport and elsewhere. The words of Ben Franklin, "Those that would give up essential liberty for temporary safety deserve neither security nor liberty", were ignored.

On top of this massive contraction of personal liberty, there is the explosive growth of technology that forces all private citizens to leave footprints of bits and bytes all over the digital landscape. The loss of the idea of any real privacy in the digital age of GPS, cell phones, and other transponders seems almost natural to many Americans. This is understandable to some extent. A side effect of this new naturally occurring data is that corporations and government are now able to monitor many aspects of our lives through the simple course of business.

From the very beginning, our Founding Fathers laid a framework for individual freedom, and the establishment was uncomfortable with it. Still without declaring martial law, the authorities could do little in 19th-century America. The land was so vast and movement so easy that keeping track of citizens was a crapshoot at best. Well into the 20th century, the cost, the lack of storage capacity, and computer processor speeds kept a lot of private information actually private, even though the government started to pass laws that made individual privacy a secondary consideration in affairs between the state and the individual. Actual 20th-century computer technologies still prevented government from infringing on privacy as much as they do in this century despite the laws.

Government, law enforcement, and corporate interests now have oodles of data on people. Many citizens are mostly unaware of just how much data is available on them. Frankly, even if people were aware, they could do little to control the distribution of the data. The government wishes to preserve its ability to monitor the citizenry and has entered into a disturbing alliance with technology companies to protect and expand this ability. Citizens must realize that the unconstitutional spying being done in this country is not to protect us from terrorists, but to allow the moneyed and powerful to protect their interests. Under the guise of security, individual liberty has been eroded by the moneyed and powerful to keep them in money and in power. A lack of individual liberty cripples change that People Power might bring.

Our country is founded on privacy and personal security for the individual. Without this personal privacy, we cease to be the America we once were. Securing the blessings of liberty for ourselves and posterity means that as technology changes, the same high bar of privacy that was achieved by our 18th-century founders is the type of privacy to be secured by the 21st-century citizen. Surely, it is more difficult in this digital age of data mining and cameras on every street corner, but achieving a real balance is a prerequisite to freedom.

Largely unsaid and unconsidered in this debate is the fact that there is so much data generated by the average citizen that there is no longer a real need for an overt surveillance society as it implicitly exists right now. After the commission of any crime, law enforcement immediately is able to access security cameras, cell phone records and countless other sources of personal data to verify alibis, which did not exist in great numbers until recently.

Rather than allowing more and more surveillance, we need to curtail its most coercive forms, because the data footprints that everyone leaves these days are sufficient to reconstruct a person's actions on any given day. Instead of providing more surveillance powers to the authorities, we should provide individual citizens with a privacy firewall that law enforcement, our government and/or corporate interests cannot pierce without court intervention. This is essential in the new century.

Progressives believe that by allowing more freedom and privacy to individuals, we will invigorate our society. Belief in freedom is not as difficult as the peddlers of fear would have us think. Looking past fear, there is still common sense. A common sense that tells us that multi-billion dollar corporations are going to protect their income streams. For example, if someone did come up with a clean cheap gasoline alternative, or a free and easy computer operating system, would not Exxon or Microsoft be very motivated to derail such a market breaking invention? Corporations with the right connections and sufficient money can monitor rivals more easily than the average citizen might think.

The CIA admits to allowing current CIA agents to moonlight for corporate interests. The CIA confirms the practice in a surprisingly unapologetic fashion. Powerful, corporate interests only pay for results, and with CIA agents having access to all kinds of backdoors to privacy, they are well paid, no doubt. Lack of privacy is bad for America and surely stifles growth and innovation. The progressive understands that an individual does have a right and a need to protect data collected about them.

Additionally, when the government can monitor dissenters so easily and completely, there is a very real, chilling effect across the whole of society. The blocking of cell phone usage to prevent a planned protest on the BART subway system of the most liberal city in the country, San Francisco, speaks to the bipartisan rollback on individual privacy. As cages are rattled in the halls of the Establishment, the databases are opened. Politicians will always use this data to quash dissent and/or political competition. Getting incriminating or just embarrassing information on your rival in an election can mean the difference between winning and losing. A crusading politician that threatens the moneyed and powerful can be easily controlled and, if necessary, rendered impotent in this day and age. Did Elliot Spitzer cross swords with too many rich and powerful individuals?

To preserve the intent of the Founding Fathers when it comes to privacy, citizens must own the data collected about them. To pass laws that the data not be collected is naïve, of course. The data exists and must be collected, if for no other reasons than to secure the blessings of convenience in the 21st-century digital age. Billing data, banking data, movement data, communication data, buying patterns, et cetera, will be collected, but the law of the land must force anonymization of a lot, if not all, of this data.

The laws should require encryption to prevent easy access to the data without keys. Those encryption keys should be in the hands of the citizen that owns the data. Individuals should have encryption technologies that prevent the searching of their personal computers without a warrant. The howls from law enforcement can drown out all reason, but we are innocent until proven guilty. Recent court cases have compelled individuals to give up passwords for such encryption technologies, but this would seem to be a clear violation of the 5th amendment. The courts have not protected privacy for the individual, but if individual juries begin to acquit defendants, then privacy is protected by the people. Another reason for progressives to support jury rights is that progressives understand that change will not come from the holders of the power.

Those with their hands on the levers of power will always use fear to put down the push for individual privacy. There will always be bank robbers, kidnappers, pedophiles, et al., that will use the tools of technology to their own nefarious ends in the same way that guns and knives can be used. Repeatedly, we are faced with the basic premise of the nation created by our Founding Fathers, which elevated the individual above the state. The Founding Fathers embraced the concept of allowing 99 guilty men go free rather than imprison 1 innocent man.

The loss of privacy in the 21st century erodes the rights of individuals and compels scared citizens to give away their own rights to the detriment to the rest of us. Only through court actions, subpoenas, search warrants, and the like, should a public key decryption be applied, overriding the individual's privacy. Individuals should always be allowed to escalate this to a jury trial, because our private data is indeed ours.

Without a doubt, these privacy rights are not being interpreted properly by our courts. Time and again, there are examples in the news of individual privacy rights being breached with no repercussions for those that breached them. For example, if our court system were not hopelessly broken, the strip search of a teenage girl for Advil would not only be seen as a violation of privacy, but a grave violation of the basic tenants of human rights and child sex laws. Nonetheless, just such a case has recently made its way through America's broken justice system. Common sense is getting scarcer in 21st-century America, and such actions by school staff led to little more than a wrist slap for the overzealous do-gooders. The aforementioned Savana Redding case went all the way to the Supreme Court, because local courts in Arizona found no illegal behavior in stripping a 13-year-old girl to search for Advil.

Though the Supreme Court eventually provided that the strip search of the teenage girl was unconstitutional, no consequences befell the perpetrators of such a heinous act. When a teenage girl's naked body cannot be protected by the Constitution and the Bill of Rights, how can some nebulous idea like virtual, digital privacy be protected? American law has strayed from common sense as it relates to privacy in the real world and the digital one. Again, it is clear that it will be the Power of the People provided through the jury and court system that will rollback these abuses of official power.

Protecting our data and privacy from the government and law enforcement is necessary for obvious reasons, but those protections need to apply to the corporate data miners too. Legislation should be sending powerful messages in the privacy laws that will force corporate owners of personal data to anonymize and provide encryption of this data by a key of the owners own choosing. Only a groundswell from a new American majority, progressives, can force lawmakers to pass such laws.

The laws will need real teeth, and corporations, government officials or individuals that violate them must face severe penalties. Penalties that have serious repercussions will be required, or the potential positive effect on the bottom line by leveraging personal data will be too difficult to resist.

For example, credit card companies control a lot of data about individual buying habits. Failures or breaches of data anonymization procedures could be penalized by forcing a credit card company to honor all usury laws in the states where they do business, immediately. These local laws typically provide for only single digit interest rates, which would seriously punish a data privacy violator. Juries should be allowed to be creative in their selection of the punishments so that the private sector truly fears entering the courtroom on charges of trafficking in personal data. Imagine the pain and suffering to their bottom lines when they fail to provide these protections. Corporations will comply, especially if juries punish them repeatedly. Over time, they will comply.

Government on the other hand, will likely continue to push their overarching right to act in the national security interest. Our government is no longer used to the idea of individual rights trumping the rights of the federal authority. The United States government believes that it has the power to wiretap all communications in the country, and so far, no court has ruled against them. Allowing the government to data mine at will is destructive to freedom.

The ACLU and EFF started to pull back the curtain on these domestic spying issues through their lawsuits against the telephone companies that aided and abetted the Bush administration's naked grab of power in 2001 before the Twin Towers attacks. However, the Obama administration helped shutdown these lawsuits by granting immunity to the telecom companies that had cooperated with the unconstitutional wiretapping. Unfortunately, the government will no longer protect individual privacy and will protect corporations from legal repercussions until their constituents loudly require a different outcome.

Citizen awareness of government actions will be the first steps toward elevating individual privacy again in this country, but only first steps, because the federal government holds many cards in the game. The U.S. government offered the telecom companies, something like $10,000 per wiretap when it embarked on its wiretapping regimen back in early 2001. The phone companies saw a big revenue stream, once they realized how extensive the government domestic spying program was going to be, so they complied.

All telecom companies complied, *except* for a company called Qwest. Qwest refused on constitutional grounds. The company was rewarded for its patriotism by the cancellation of government contracts that it had already secured. Of course, the owner could see his stock price was going to fall in this battle, and he ended up selling some of his shares, quite logically. The government tried and convicted him for insider trading. He is now serving time in prison. Coincidence or retribution, you decide.

The government is in a position to either bribe or bully a corporation into complying. It should be obvious to the progressive that courtroom rebukes brought by free juries are the only path. It is foolish to believe that the data miners are going to concentrate on protecting citizens when there are so many other profitable uses for the data. What was the SEC up to at the beginning of this century, because they obviously were not watching AIG and the rest of the financial robber barons, as a financial collapse was looming? One has to wonder why Martha Stewart was so important to prosecute, while the entire banking system was being looted. Perhaps she annoyed a powerful person at some party, and the SEC was used to punish her "disrespectful" behavior. This would be a predicted outcome of corporate and government snooping.

Ask yourself, why with the level of data mining going on, how did Bernie Madoff make off with billions, while Martha Stewart landed in prison? Ask yourself, why Ted Kennedy was stopped at the airport for years after September 11, 2001, for having a name similar to a terrorist on the watch list? Without individual privacy, we lose our freedom and strength. Repeatedly, we can see privacy data being used for revenge and political or financial gain, not the preservation of justice. Individuals should understand that a government that does not respect individual privacy does not make them safer, but rather, it puts them at risk for revenge, persecution, and oppression of the worst kind.

Honoring the Bill of Rights

We have spent a number of pages harping on individual freedom, the Constitution, and the Bill of Rights. Many may feel that this is exaggerating the unconstitutional behavior of our government, including the highly politicized Supreme Court. Constitutional interpretations are meant to evolve, but the Supreme Court seems to no longer protect individual rights. The Supreme Court seems to be allied with the other branches of government and no longer acting as the check on the other two as it should.

For example, to stop the sale of previously legal alcohol in America, an amendment to the Constitution was passed that started Prohibition. Years later, yet another amendment was required to repeal Prohibition. Strangely, though, shortly after this repeal, Prohibition was restarted without any bothersome constitutional amendments. The banning of the legal sale and use of marijuana did *not* require an amendment to the Constitution just a few years after Prohibition had been repealed. Why? What changed? Consider the continued bypassing of the Constitution behavior after WWII, while you read on about the Bill of Rights.

In this section, let us look at each of the first ten amendments to the Constitution and show how they have been watered down or practically repealed in today's America. America is struggling, and we must return to our roots to save ourselves. Progressives cannot reiterate enough that we must uphold the constitutional rights of our citizens if we are going to be free and return to greatness. Freedom is messy, but it also brings vitality and security in ways that often are not immediately clear.

Progressives must urge Americans to quit being so afraid and stop expecting the police to protect them from any and all harm. We now know that unconstitutional wiretapping was actually begun by the Bush administration almost immediately upon seizing the mantle of power in January 2001. However, these new extra-constitutional powers failed to allow the same administration to detect and prevent the terrorism of September 11, 2001. As the Founding Fathers clearly understood, such extra-constitutional powers would surely be used by those in power to preserve their power, not protect free citizens. Power corrupts, and without the proper checks and balances, our government can do as it pleases— which it often does.

Here it is, the most progressive AND radical of all American documents, the Bill of Rights.

First Amendment – Establishment Clause, Free Exercise Clause; freedom of speech, of the press, and of assembly; right to petition. *Congress shall make no law respecting an establishment of religion, or prohibiting the free exercise thereof; or abridging the freedom of speech, or of the press; or the right of the people peaceably to assemble, and to petition the Government for a redress of grievances.*

There has been a chilling effect on this amendment, and it is hard to know where to start. The Supreme Court ruling, giving more and more "person" rights to corporations, has been one of the reasons for this. As corporations have gained personal rights, corporations have been able to suppress speech by using their deep pockets to sue individuals for speaking out. Additionally, freedom of the press has all but disappeared with the aggregation of media in all forms by large corporations. Large corporations are not truly interested in protecting citizen rights, muckraking, or other such altruistic motives. Corporations are motivated by preserving and increasing profit margins. Once it was impossible to own most, if not all, media outlets in one media market, let alone the entire country, but corporate-written legislation has erased these restrictions.

Television journalism has degraded seriously over the years to become more of an entertainment outlet. We as a people truly have a stake in National Public Radio and the Corporation for Public Broadcasting. These journalistic arms of the people have been seriously curtailed by a lack of funding. We must restore funding to the Vox Populi outlets to prevent all investigative reporting being subject to whims of corporate power. The demise of print media has made it even more essential for journalism to receive public funding to keep politicians in check. Freedom of the Press is not a bad thing, though many conservatives have demonized it since the days of Watergate.

First Amendment abridgements do not stop there either. Again and again, the government has also reduced free assembly and speech rights to quell dissent on the street during WTO or IMF meetings as well as during political rallies, especially for the party in power. The 1st Amendment no longer seems to be as strongly embraced by the government or the people, but it is a keystone in our republic.

Second Amendment – Right to keep and bear arms. *A well-regulated Militia, being necessary to the security of a free State, the right of the people to keep and bear Arms, shall not be infringed.*

The second amendment seems rather straightforward. People have the right to keep and bear arms for their personal protection as well as for the maintenance of an independent militia not tied to the federal government. Many would argue that gun control laws are a progressive thing, but individual citizen power requires the 2nd amendment. Power to the People must also mean the power to own a weapon. Progressives believe that crime would be reduced if criminals feared that their potential victim might be armed. Breaking into a person's home could become rather dangerous for burglars when individuals are more likely to shoot the perpetrator in the act.

Progressives realize that it is just not criminals breaking into homes nowadays. The 2nd amendment helps to curtail police power as well. Breaking down doors of citizens might be a bit more dangerous. Police may have more motivation to present their search warrants before searching a residence, rather than simply storming in armed to the teeth. The number of individuals dying at the hands of police is not small. More and more those victims are turning out to be innocents that police accidentally killed. This is unacceptable in a free society.

Apologies to liberals, but freedom is not free, and free citizens must be allowed to protect themselves and not simply depend on the government to do so. This does not mean that progressives believe there should be no licensing or background checks. Individuals are not allowed to drive cars in this country without some modicum of training. Guns are just as dangerous as cars and some type of licensing should be instituted as a matter of public safety. Additionally, felons should also be prevented from obtaining weapons. To accomplish these goals, a minimal background check and a waiting period does not seem to be a violation of this amendment.

Again, progressives must find the common ground between the battling of *isms* in this country in order to bring the people and the nation together to protect the abridgement of citizen rights on arms.

Third Amendment – Protection from quartering of troops. *No Soldier shall, in time of peace, be quartered in any house, without the consent of the Owner, nor in time of war, but in a manner to be prescribed by law.*

Of the ten amendments first added to the Constitution, this is the one that seems the most archaic—over 200 years and a 90% hit rate by our Founding Fathers. What a record! It's one that our current lawmakers could only dream of achieving. This amendment was a direct result of the British government quartering soldiers within the homes of colonists before and during the Revolutionary War. However, such things could return today, given the increasing power of the Federal government to use the military within the borders of the US in direct violation of the Posse Comitatus Act.

Fourth Amendment – Protection from unreasonable search and seizure. *The right of the people to be secure in their persons, houses, papers, and effects, against unreasonable searches and seizures, shall not be violated, and no Warrants shall issue, but upon probable cause, supported by Oath or affirmation, and particularly describing the place to be searched, and the persons or things to be seized.*

This right has been largely repealed through fear, and more and more believe that the government has the right to protect us from ourselves. The security theater that has been instituted in our airports is in direct violation of this amendment. There has been no proof that this has made anyone safer. It was not 9/11 that put the fourth amendment under assault, but rather the sobriety checkpoints backed by MADD and other protect-us-from-ourselves groups. Perhaps, just perhaps, there were public safety issues that allowed the sobriety checkpoints, but the checkpoints opened the door to all kinds of other types of checkpoints. The checkpoints have been widely expanded to include seat belt checkpoints, registration checkpoints, and baby car seat checkpoints. Of course, if any illegal activity is turned up, it can be used against an individual, and usually, a search is justified by a dog.

The War on Drugs justified all kinds of constitutional abuses. Once these abridgements to the fourth amendment were forced through, they were broadened widely in the name of the War on Terror, and the fourth amendment seems to be just a memory. The amendment's reference to "effects" could easily be interpreted to include one's "digital effects". Not surprisingly, judges and courts have not pinned this down as they should have by now.

Fifth Amendment – Due process, double jeopardy, self-incrimination, eminent domain. *No person shall be held to answer for any capital, or otherwise infamous crime, unless on a presentment or indictment of a Grand Jury, except in cases arising in the land or naval forces, or in the Militia, when in actual service in time of War or public danger; nor shall any person be subject for the same offence to be twice put in jeopardy of life or limb; nor shall be compelled in any criminal case to be a witness against himself, nor be deprived of life, liberty, or property, without due process of law; nor shall private property be taken for public use, without just compensation.*

The Fifth Amendment has been largely repealed as well. As noted in the chapter on jury nullification, the federal government's prosecution of the LAPD officers in the Rodney King case appeared to violate the double jeopardy clause of this amendment. However, that is the least of the violations of this amendment. Asset forfeiture laws in this nation have gone completely out of control since they were first used to prosecute drug dealers in the 1980s. Constitutionally, assets cannot be seized without due process in this amendment, yet the government regularly does so in a whole host of situations nowadays. The original basis for such asset forfeiture laws is shaky. Originally, it was to prevent drug dealers from paying for good lawyers.

However, to the progressive, criminals having their ill-gotten gains to pay for lawyers should not be a serious advantage, if the state actually has evidence of such crimes, except in the most extraordinary circumstances, one would expect a conviction to be obtained. Asset forfeiture is now being used to further fund law enforcement entities in a clear conflict of interest. For most of the last decade, the Bureau of Alcohol Tobacco and Firearms has used the slogan, "Always Think Forfeiture". They in fact had the slogan on BATF swag until very recently. None of these forfeitures of assets ever requires due process. Law enforcement personnel determine whether assets are to be seized at the moment of arrest, and this is not what the Founding Fathers meant by due process.

Sixth Amendment – Trial by jury and rights of the accused; Confrontation Clause, speedy trial, public trial, right to counsel. *In all criminal prosecutions, the accused shall enjoy the right to a speedy and public trial, by an impartial jury of the State and district where in the crime shall have been committed, which district shall have been previously ascertained by law, and to be informed of the nature and cause of the accusation; to be confronted with the witnesses against him; to have compulsory process for obtaining witnesses in his favor, and to have the Assistance of Counsel for his defense.*

When faced with a trial, to have one's assets seized would seriously hinder one's ability to secure Assistance of Counsel. Having a jury pool that is so scarce also makes it quite difficult for the accused to really be tried by peers, but rather only by people with sufficient assets already to be able to afford to sit in judgment. The state has now begun to introduce things like "secret evidence" and use testimony of paid informants to convict individuals.

We have not even touched on this new concept of an enemy combatant, originally put forward by the Bush Administration. The Supreme Court has so far let the idea stand that these enemy combatants do not need to be treated as normal arrestees worthy of due process, nor do they need to be given POW status and the rights accorded to them via the Geneva Convention.

The idea that the U.S. can indefinitely detain individuals without charge, without trial, and torture them is sickening. Progressives love America, and believe we are the good guys. Torturing people and throwing them in prison forever is not what the good guys do. Of course, these are not American citizens, so a case has been made that the Constitution does not apply. Progressives though see America as a place where basic human dignity is respected through due process of law regardless of citizenship.

Progressives understand the consequences of allowing our government to treat non-citizens poorly. There are several lines of argument today that assert the President somehow has the power to label an American citizen as an enemy combatant, and therefore, that person loses all Constitutional protections. Citizens need to wake up to the incredible danger of such power; it gives the President the powers of a dictator or a king. Beware of offending a person with such power, because you can become a non-person, non-citizen and prisoner at the stroke of a pen.

Seventh Amendment – Civil trial by jury. *In suits at common law, where the value in controversy shall exceed twenty dollars, the right of trial by jury shall be preserved, and no fact tried by a jury, shall be otherwise re-examined in any court of the United States, than according to the rules of the common law.*

The rules of common law denigrated today are really the basis of everything! The U.S. is a common law country. In all states, except Louisiana (which is based on the French civil code), the common law of England was adopted as the general law of the state, *except* when a statute provides otherwise. Common law has no statutory basis; judges establish common law through written opinions that are binding on future decisions of lower courts in the same jurisdiction. Broad areas of the law, most notably relating to property, contracts, and torts are traditionally part of the common law. These areas of the law are mostly within the jurisdiction of the states, and thus, state courts are the primary source of common law. Common law is used to fill in gaps.

Common law changes over time, and at this time, each state has its own common law on many topics. The area of federal common law is primarily limited to federal issues that have not been addressed by a statute. Though this amendment is meant to support the idea of Jury Nullification, as previously stated, such voting of conscience is no longer permitted in America.

Eighth Amendment – Prohibition of excessive bail and cruel and unusual punishment. *Excessive bail shall not be required, nor excessive fines imposed, nor cruel and unusual punishments inflicted.*

The current state of our prison system now constitutes cruel and unusual punishment. Prison overcrowding is a serious issue nationwide. These issues are real and not to be diminished. To force individuals into cramped quarters where they are often subjected to all manner of sexual abuse is clearly cruel and unusual. Yet, our fearful society continues to pass laws and resist reform to reduce prison overcrowding. We imprison a greater number and percentage of our population than any Western nation. Imagine the potential of so many of these people thrown on the scrap heap by our overzealous law-and-order mentality.

Ninth Amendment – Protection of rights not specifically enumerated in the Bill of Rights. *The enumeration in the Constitution, of certain rights, shall not be construed to deny or disparage others retained by the people.*

Judicial activism is often rooted in this amendment, meant to protect the rights of individuals. Our crazy "make a new law" society has largely sprung up with our desire to curtail the broader rights of individuals that should be protected here. We need to step back from this and reevaluate whether it is wise to give so much power to the police by making so much illegal. This caveat is especially germane as it relates to those laws that criminalize crimes against ourselves, such as drugs, not wearing seat belts, etc.

Tenth Amendment – Powers of states and people.

The powers not delegated to the United States by the Constitution, nor prohibited by it to the states, are reserved to the states respectively, or to the people.

Again, this amendment clearly means to preserve the rights of individuals, but our fearful society cannot seem to embrace these ideals. We spend far too much time making laws to abridge individuals rights, and therefore, we constrain free citizens from their constitutionally protected right to pursue life, liberty, and the pursuit of happiness.

And so there we are a breakdown of the Bill of Rights for the progressive thinker.

But wait! There were actually twelve articles in the first draft of the Bill of Rights, and only articles 3 through 12 were ratified. Here is the text of the missing amendments that were to make up the original Bill of Rights:

Article II – On Congressional pay. *No law varying the compensation for the services of the Senators and Representatives shall take effect, until an election of Representatives shall have intervened.*

This provided protection against congressional pay hikes, preventing a sitting Congress from giving itself a raise. Any increase in pay would not go into effect until the following House election. This proposal was resurrected 203 years later when it became the 27th amendment to the Constitution in 1992! Again, the Founding Fathers predicted situations and provided a statutory basis to address the situation—such foresight!

Article I – Providing for a truly representative republican democracy. *After the first enumeration required by the first article of the Constitution, there shall be one representative for every thirty thousand, until the number shall amount to one hundred, after which the proportion shall be so regulated by Congress, that there shall be not less than one hundred representatives, nor less than one representative for every forty thousand persons, until the number of representatives shall amount to two hundred; after which the proportion shall be so regulated by Congress, that there shall be not less than two hundred representatives, nor more than one representative for every fifty thousand persons.*

The explosive growth of our population outstripped these visionary representation numbers. This was followed on by the abolition of slavery and women's suffrage, which changed the demographic electoral equations dramatically. Nonetheless, the

Founding Fathers expected the House of Representatives to continue to grow with the growth of the electorate. Inexplicably, for a century we have been stuck at a little more than 400 representatives!

Hmmm.....

Size of the U.S. House of Representatives

The House of Representatives was meant to be the People's House. Despite popular belief, America is not a democracy, but rather a representative republic. That means that our representatives, who are democratically elected over set periods, do the government's business as representative proxies. At the beginning of our republic, to get each of the states to sign on to the new Constitution, each was given two votes in the Senate, despite the size of their populations, thereby making sure that each state was equal in that representative body. However, clearly, for America to be a true representative republic, there had to be a legislative body that was based upon population. That body was the House of Representatives.

The framers of the Constitution and the Bill of Rights intended that the total population of Congressional districts should never exceed 50 to 60 thousand. Currently, the average population size of the districts is nearly 700,000. George Washington agreed that the original representation proposed in the Constitutional Convention (one representative for every 40,000) was inadequate and supported an alteration to reduce that number to 30,000. This was the only time that Washington expressed an opinion on any of the actual issues debated during the convention.

In Federalist No. 55, James Madison addressed the claims that the representation would be inadequate by stating that the major inadequacies would be cured over time by virtue of decennial reapportionment based upon the census. Madison was acknowledging that there were some inadequacies at the House level in the original Constitution, but that every ten years the census would allow for adjustments. Madison expected these inadequacies eventually to go away, not to be made worse or set in stone by the central government.

For some reason, in the early 20th century, our government abandoned the principle of proportionally equitable representation. Prior to the 20th century, the number of representatives increased every decade as more states joined the union and the population increased. In 1911, Public Law 62-5 raised the membership of the U.S. House to 433 with a provision to add one permanent seat each upon the admissions of Arizona and New Mexico as states. As provided, membership increased to 435 in 1912. But, in 1921, Congress failed to reapportion the House membership as required by the United States Constitution. Then, in 1929, Congress passed the Reapportionment Act of 1929, which capped the size of the House at 435, and we have been stuck at this 435 number ever since.

This inadequate representation from the early 20th century has only gotten more inadequate. The U.S. population has increased rapidly, and the membership of the House of Representatives has stayed static. Obviously, the population increase that has occurred since the early 20th century warrants change. Change is essential, in light of the fact that the actual number of eligible voters doubled with women receiving the vote at about the same time that the number of representatives was frozen at 435. The current size of 435 seats means one member represents on average about 650,000 people; but exact representation per member varies by state. Four states – Wyoming, Vermont, Alaska, and North Dakota – have populations smaller than the average for a single district.

Many would argue that the size of the House is one of practicality. That increasing the number of members would create chaos and nothing would ever be done in Congress. Progressives would argue that there is not much "positive and useful" being done right now, so how can the status quo be advocated? The changes progressives advocate in our society and in our system seem quite dramatic, even though much of them are based on the original precepts of our nation. It is quite illustrative of how far we have strayed from the original ideas of our founders that arguing to a return to our basic principles would seem so revolutionary.

We do need to increase the size of the House; there is no question about that. It is only a matter of how much to increase it by. Let us address the objection that more than 435 would be impossible to manage. First, we should consider the amount of

Congressional staff each representative has. If these non-elected staffers were eliminated or at least capped, it would free up quite a bit of space for real representatives of the people as well as money to pay those new representatives. Also, technology has advanced to the point that video conferencing truly is almost as good as being there.

Opponents should consider that other democracies seem to get by with more than 435 members without chaos ensuing. The parliament that was one of the first people's bodies in the western world, the House of Commons in Britain, has more than 600 members, as does the Bundestag in Germany, another great western democracy. These parliamentary bodies serve populations that are one-fifth the size of our population, yet they are almost 50% larger! Surely, we have fallen behind the curve of representative democracy.

Progressives should strongly support an initial doubling of the size of the House of Representatives based upon the current 2010 census. We should then consider doubling it again in the 2020 census or increasing it by 50% over five year intervals leading to 2020. This would still leave us far short of the original vision of our founders. A case could even be made to continuing to increase the size of the House of Representatives until a 1 to 50,000 ratio was achieved.

A smaller ratio of people to representative could lead to more than one thousand House of Representatives members and dramatically increase the payroll of our government, but that's a small price to pay. We would actually begin to immunize our House of Representatives from the corruptions of money. With so many votes to swing a majority, it would become ever more impractical to influence the House via lobbyist money. There would also be an increase in the number of voices that would be heard on the national stage. Our country has stagnated, and the solutions to our problems seem insoluble only because of the narrowness of the vision of those in politics today.

Indeed, if there ever was to be a new and electable 3rd party, for example, the Progressives, this increase would begin the process of giving these new political voices an opportunity to be heard. Sure, we may have to build a new legislative building, but such is the price of freedom. As we have seen, our government has had no problem finding money to finance foreign wars or bailout too big to fail banks. The money that our government has printed in these endeavors cannot be characterized as investments, but are actually bailouts and wartime profiteering. Progressives believe that the whole point of spending money on this new larger House of Representatives is that it is a true investment. An investment in a game-changing vision that will return our citizens to their rightful place in American leadership is worth the money. Currently, our leadership has run our country into the ground, and an increase in the size of the House of Representatives helps return the reins of power to the people.

America, in God We Trust

Somehow, many Americans have forgotten that the U.S. Constitution is a secular document. It begins, "We the people...", and contains no mention of "God" or "Christianity". The only references to religion are exclusionary, for example, "no religious test shall ever be required as a qualification to any office or public trust" (Article VI). and "Congress shall make no law respecting an establishment of religion, or prohibiting the free exercise thereof" (First Amendment). The presidential oath of office, the only oath detailed in the Constitution, does not contain the phrase "so help me God" or any requirement to swear on a Bible (Article II, Section 1, Clause 8). If we were born a Christian nation, surely our Constitution would explicitly say so.

Christians will cite that the early colonies had established churches and that the government actively supported Christianity. This argument is not effective, because it was exactly this situation against which many early Americans fought. Colony governments did support Christianity in many cases, but only the sect of Christianity to which they subscribed. Jefferson's fight for the Baptists in Virginia was specifically about the right of the Baptists to practice their religion in Virginia, even though to Jefferson the Baptists were superstitious and backward.

The First Amendment was specifically designed to prohibit government established churches, and at the Constitutional Convention, attempts to write in some sort of specific support for Christianity always failed. The Founding Fathers opposed such an establishment based upon their own experiences. Objective historians note that people at the time of the American Revolution were not avid churchgoers. The best estimates indicate that only 10% to 15% of the population actually attended church services in 18th century America.

Sometimes Ben Franklin is dragged into this debate despite his very secular nature. Few will deny that Ben Franklin proposed that delegates at the Constitutional Convention open their sessions with morning prayers. Christian zealots who oppose the separation of church often make a big deal of this. The records of the time do support that Franklin suggested, "Henceforth prayers imploring the assistance of Heaven, and its blessing on our deliberations, be held in this Assembly every morning before we proceed to business."

The prayer isn't specifically Christian, and on further research from the records of the time, one finds that his proposal was never accepted. In fact, delegates didn't even bother voting on it, but rather, they voted to adjourn for the day. Finally, Franklin never bothered to mention it again. Accounts of the day portray Ben Franklin's original proposal as borne out of frustration and indignation at the lack of progress and not meant to be taken seriously. The fallacy that America was born a Christian nation is thwarted by the Founding Fathers' refusal to base this nation on Christianity which can be seen in the fact that neither God nor Christianity are mentioned anywhere in the Constitution.

Once formed, the United States went on and specifically stated that it was not a Christian nation. The occasion was a peace and trade agreement between the United States and Muslim leaders in North Africa. The original negotiations were conducted under the authority of George Washington. The Senate under the leadership of John Adams, the second president, approved of the final document, known as the Treaty of Tripoli. This treaty states, without equivocation, that the "...Government of the United States is not, in any sense, founded on the Christian religion..." None can argue the piety of John Adams, but even his strong Christian beliefs did not prevent him from signing the treaty into the law of the land.

Activist Christian politicians would have us believe that America was founded as a Christian nation, which was then later subverted by godless liberals and humanists. Just the opposite is the case, however. The Constitution is a secular document and the government of the United States was set up as a formally secular nation. It would seem more accurate to portray well-meaning Christians as subverting our nation's founding secular principles.

Importantly, progressives should note the well-meaning aspect of this subversion. Because most Americans are Christians, they often do not see the potential evil they do by forcing their beliefs into our nation's government. Our Founding Fathers, without a doubt, were spiritual men, most of them Christians, but their desire to keep religion out of politics is clear from close examination of the documents that frame our government.

There is a reason that the first amendment of the Constitution in the Bill of Rights contains the following: "Congress shall make no law respecting an establishment of religion, or prohibiting the free exercise thereof..." Most of the religious colonial governments actually persecuted those of the wrong faith and had an official Christian sect. Massachusetts probably hung more people for being Quaker than it did for being witches. The framers of our Constitution in 1787 wanted no part of religious intolerance and bloodshed, wisely establishing the first government in history to separate church and state.

The words "separation of church and state" do not appear in the Constitution, admittedly. President Thomas Jefferson coined the phrase, "a wall of separation between church and state." It appears in a letter to the Danbury Baptists in 1802, when they had asked him to explain the First Amendment. The Supreme Court, and lower courts, have used Jefferson's phrase repeatedly in major decisions upholding neutrality in matters of religion. Thomas Jefferson, explaining the phrase to the Danbury Baptists, felt that personal religious views are just that, personal. Our society cannot be based on these highly personal beliefs. Only theocracy can come from Christians who continue their agitation for a return to a historical tradition of religiosity that never existed.

The most official seeming religious references in American society are actually the most recent and do not even date back to the 19th century, let alone the 18th century. The words "under God" did not appear in the Pledge of Allegiance until 1954, when Congress, under the spell of McCarthyism, inserted them. Likewise, "In God We Trust" was absent from paper currency before 1956. It only appeared on some coins earlier, as did other sundry phrases, such as 'Mind Your Business." The original U.S. motto, chosen by John Adams, Benjamin Franklin, and Thomas

Jefferson, is E Pluribus Unum ("Of Many, One"), celebrating plurality, not theocracy.

Despite Judeo-Christian protestations, American law is not based on the Ten Commandments. The first four Commandments are religious edicts, having nothing to do with law or ethical behavior. Only three (homicide, theft, and perjury) are relevant to current American law, and those have existed in cultures long before Moses. If Americans honored the commandment against coveting, free enterprise would collapse! The Supreme Court has ruled repeatedly that posting the Ten Commandments in public schools is unconstitutional, though one wonders whether today's court might overturn this.

Why be concerned about the separation of church and state? Ignoring history, law, and fairness, many fanatics are working vigorously to turn America into a Christian nation. History shows us that only harm comes from uniting church and state. Our secular laws, based on the human principle of justice for all, provide protection against crimes, and our civil government enforces them through a secular criminal justice system.

No one is deprived of worship in America. Tax-exempt churches and temples are everywhere, and tax-exempt institutions engaging in highly political arenas in support of a specific party are damaging the social balance. The actions of these institutions should invalidate such tax exemptions. The state has no say about private religious beliefs and practices, unless they endanger health or life. Our government represents all of the people, supported by dollars, from a plurality of religious and non-religious taxpayers.

America is supposed to be a place where the Christian and the pagan can have an honest conversation about their religious beliefs without it mattering politically. The twisting of science for political ends has accelerated this pushing of religion into the public sector. Science must be a part of our decision-making process as a society, but religion really has no official place. Of course, it is clear that it affects the moral judgments of individuals, but that is personal not institutional religion.

Science should not be considered a religion and should not be seen as hostile to religion, but science has become very political in America. Scientists are too closely tied to corporate and governmental revenue streams to be trustworthy on many issues of political import. Americans, religious or not, have to be able to interpret data for themselves via the tried and true scientific method. Americans cannot continue denying scientific facts due to a perceived hostility toward one's religion. The growing belief that science is just another religion does not help America succeed in this very scientific and technological world.

Specific Policy

Policy Wonk

Government of the people, by the people and for the people can only function effectively when those people participate. We have reached a point where people need to get involved in a grand scale. The French Revolution's Reign of Terror must be a cautionary tale to all who advocate power for the people, though. To prevent a mob mentality, the citizenry must have a broad unifying vision of the future path. Without this unifying vision, the majority cannot stay together. We the People are just that, simply people, subject to all of our character flaws, vanities and prejudices. These natural character flaws of the people will always be exploited by the oligarchs to keep the people separate and hostile to each other.

We the People can all agree that murder should be illegal, because the issues are so clear that nearly all of us arrive at the same conclusion. Similarly, when the requirement for driver's licenses and the institution of traffic laws came about due to the invention of the car, we quickly came together on solutions. There were obvious potential problems caused by free citizens driving around the countryside in control of so much mechanical power and weight. This consensus that permitted efficient law making now escapes us.

The 21st century has made things very complicated and money-fueled partisanship keeps the picture cloudy. This cloudiness virtually guarantees very little is done. With a stake in the bipartisan firefight, money will drive the parties to opposite corners of an issue.

An understanding of problems to be addressed is an absolute necessity for the power of people to be brought to bear on any given issue. People must understand the issues of the day clearly to stay together and resist divisive propaganda. Here is where the 21st century has really made things complicated. For people power to function, a broad agreement on the facts of a given issue is necessary. Today it is ever more difficult to get at these facts. This makes it easier for moneyed power to cloud a given issue and deny consensus.

There is no denying that the power of the people can simply lead to chaos. Therefore if this book is to do any good, it must lay out some specific policy positions on the wedge issues that are keeping Americans from coming together on our mounting list of problems. These specific policy positions are meant to layout a middle ground that the Silent Majority can easily occupy without wavering. We need common sense solutions to problems that have seemed so intractable over the decades of warfare between liberals and conservatives.

Environmental policy is a good place to start, because it has so clearly been manipulated by partisanship to the point of lunacy that it should help the reader see through the noise of the last couple of decades. The global climate has been a huge American advantage since the beginning. Once Americans see how partisanship has prevented us from preserving this advantage, it should help the reader realize how important it is for people power to come to the aid of our nation. Also, since it was environmental issues that made me break with the left/right axis twenty years ago, it seems appropriate to start-off with it to help my fellow Americans make the same break.

The Partisan Divide Worsens Global Climate Change

There is no question that fanatical environmentalism has had a hand in the public's eroded belief in the scientific community. Many predictions of disaster permeated scientific opinion in the 1970s, and much of it did not come to be true. In addition, some feel good liberal analysis of social problems during this decade, based on so-called hard social science, cast doubt on the real hard sciences like biology, botany, and physics, to name a few. The softer social sciences were used to justify expensive, yet ineffective, social programs. This helped substantiate some of society's growing doubts about science in general. Finally, the political conflict over global climate change made science appear even more confused as both proponents and opponents were able to pay for scientific opinions and data to support their political positions.

To the public, so-called hard science has begun to look like an opinion and not a factual measure of the real world. Coupled with a greater religious zeal that snuck into the public sector more and more during the 20th century, science became ever more suspect. The battle over global climate change and what to do about it really made Americans skeptical of scientists. Scientists seemed to be saying just what they were paid to say. The public's faith in science as a bottom line to cut through political passions was broken. The theory of evolution, once considered an unassailable fact, has been questioned due to a waning belief in science and a growing embrace of evangelical Christianity among mainstream society. Pouring gasoline on the fire, political parties have fostered the conflict between science and religion for their own gain.

Essentially, Republicans have been able to reap large benefits by identifying with the evangelical Christian constituency.

Republicans had an instant grassroots revolution based upon the myth that the United States was founded as a Christian Nation and that the evil liberal Democrats have taken America from her traditional roots.

This war between religion and science has been generally unproductive for our country, but it has brought about a Republican resurgence since the Nixon presidency. This is just another example of partisanship ignoring the nation's needs to promote its electability.

For years, conservative Republicans have been denying global climate change even existed. The Republican embrace of the evangelicals allowed them to leverage the constituency's mistrust of science to bring into doubt that human activity was changing the global climate. Along with this scientific distrust, semantics got in the way too. Twenty years ago, global climate change was widely known as global warming. That was a real misnomer and helped cloud the issue to the delight of the skeptics. Any time there was a harsh winter storm or severe bouts of cold weather, the jokes would fill the air about "Global warming? What global warming?"

Nonetheless, global climate change was happening twenty years ago and it is clear that it continues to happen now. However, with evangelicals convinced that science is anti-Christian and Republicans supporting that view, it means that there is more doubt today about global climate change than there was two decades ago. The right portrays most proposed solutions to global climate change as hippies trying to roll back America's technological society to some nature-worshipping commune.

The right claims that it wants to make policy on hard science and not on political rhetoric, but science supports manmade global climate change. Giant blizzards engulfing the US in the winter have strengthened the cries of, "What global warming?" and bred more skepticism from the right as well as the average American on the street. These blizzards actually are supportive of global climate change if one understands the science behind it.

This distrust of science is bad for America and humanity in general. Science is not inherently evil, but rather a tool. Just as a gun, might be used to kill a teenager in a drive by, it can also stop a rapist before the act. The scientific method is a tool and not some great mystery. Science requires testable and repeatable experiments. When such experiments are not easily created and replicated, there is definitely room for debate. However, in the case of global climate change much of that debate revolves around just how dramatic and how fast the global climate is changing, not whether it is changing. The reality that there still exists reasoned debate among climate scientists is used by the naysayers to promote their wait and see arguments.

Weather still defies our computer models to make long-term accurate predictions. This is due to the extraordinary amount of data that needs to be processed. Unfortunately, we are still years away from achieving processing speeds that allow us to collect data and crunch the numbers in time to beat the occurrence of the weather. Nonetheless, it is clear that the Earth's weather is a large heat driven equation and as the numbers being entered into the equation get bigger one can expect ever more giant swings in the output as well as greater unpredictability. In lay terms, understanding this basic aspect of the equations defining weather models means one could expect colder winters, hotter summers, more and more violent hurricanes and tornadoes along with a good deal of unexpected variability with greater heat factors being applied to the equation.

Exactly how this will all play out is still beyond our technology to predict, but that does not mean we should take no action and simply ignore the situation. Over the years, both sides of the debate have taken advantage of the uncertainty of future weather predictions and been able to field their set of scientists and experts backing their point of view. It is one of the reasons why the decision to take action has been put off for so long. There seemed to be no conclusive evidence.

Tragically muddying the water as well is the traditional environmentalist lobby, which has backed their own scientific studies and been caught skewing facts on some occasions. Traditional environmentalist solutions often fail to take into account some basic pragmatic realities. Unfortunately, many of the environmentalist-sponsored models cannot be considered anything more than guesses due to uncertainties about the historical data and difficulty collecting real time data in the present. Yes, global climate change is real, but exactly how it will all work out in the end is speculation. That is the true hard science on the matter and the actions we take must be flexible. The climate is changing and at least some of that change is directly related to human activity, specifically the burning of fossil fuels.

How much of the change is arguable for sure, but current temperature swings are swinging beyond historical variations. The thawing of the ancient iceboxes in the south and north of the planet are real. Such thawing will open a Northwest Passage to be plied by the world's merchant sailors soon. Countries like Tuvalu in the South Pacific are struggling to keep their heads above water, literally, as sea level rise begins to shrink their flat coral atoll of a country to nothing. Venice is building a vast complex of storm doors and sea walls to protect their city from global sea level rise. The British are also spending enormous amounts of money to protect London from storm surges coming up the Thames. Oil companies are investing billions in preparation for an ice-free Artic that can be drilled. The investment of REAL BIG dollars says global climate change is happening.

Another thing that is abundantly clear is that historically America has been blessed with an advantageous climate. We have been able to feed ourselves, and much of the world, via our vast tracts of arable land. In fact, one of America's deepest and darkest times was definitely related to the black blizzards of the Great Depression's Dust Bowl blighting these same vast tracts of arable land. We cannot be sure about how things will work out in the climate change roulette the world has begun. Perhaps things will work out in America's favor, but the odds are long that changes to the climate will preserve this inherent American advantage. After all, change means just that, change, and we can hardly afford any degradation to our current advantage.

Afford is what we will somehow have to do as weather related disasters bleed our nation's economic resources. Already hurricanes appear to be increasing in number due to the greater heat input into the atmosphere. These destructive storms also appear to be becoming more powerful. Tornados also appear to be on the increase in the breadbasket of America. Whether these trends will continue, no one can be sure, but the odds would seem to favor their continuation. The greater heat input is just like putting bigger numbers into the aforementioned climate modeling equations. Those equations predict greater heat input would create greater variability and unpredictability and that appears to be accurate.

The denial of these scientific facts, which are all pointing to one conclusion, "human industrial activity is affecting global climate", represents a great failure of conservatism, not to mention the world of science as well. Conservatives found it far too easy to recruit scientists that could spin the numbers in ways that made out global climate change to be nothing more than normal permutations of the Earth's climate or the sun's output. If scientists had been less easy to recruit on this matter, perhaps things would have worked out differently, but it seems money can buy anything, including scientific facts.

The corruptions of money and corporate power have deformed our society horribly not just on this issue, but also on many more. Corporations control much of the research dollars and, therefore, the livelihood of scientists. That makes getting the scientific data the corporate lobbyists needed was just a matter of writing checks. Now, in the 21st century, it is very easy to blame conservatives and corporations for this stunning failure to act upon the obvious, but that answer is far too easy. Ordinary Americans really wanted to believe these spin-doctoring scientists, since gas was cheap in the 1990s, and tooling around in a big SUV is fun. Progressives must admit that Americans cannot continuously blame politicians for chasing the money when we as citizens provide so little coherent guidance. Citizens are or should be the power of this nation, and it is high time we stepped up to the plate.

Another reason we are tackling the environmental issues as our first specific policy position is that these are the most scientifically verifiable issues of our time. Competing ideologies have muddied the clarity of environmental issues. Average citizens need to book up on the scientific method, so that they can do some interpretation on their own of data relating to climate change and a whole host of other complicated issues. Progressives must help educate the people on the global climate change issue and help drive consensus on solutions. To do this, progressives will need to take on the traditionally Democratic and liberal environmental lobby not just the Republican and conservative lobby. Progressives must understand how liberals exacerbated global climate change by stalling the most effective solution to the problem.

Many conservative readers of this text may be amused by the irony that my big break with liberalism back in 1989 was due to my tree-hugging nature. The next chapter was originally titled, <u>What a Tree Whispered to Me</u>, when I first tried to urge public action on the global climate change issue over 20 years ago.

Pro-Nuclear Environmentalism

The idea of a pro-nuclear environmentalist is an oxymoron to many. The events in Japan at Fukushima seem to have killed nuclear power as an energy option...again...just as Chernobyl and Three Mile Island did back in the 1980s. The climate environment has deteriorated to such an extent that this position is no longer tenable when one considers all the facts, even in light of Fukushima. Nuclear power is our last hope of maintaining a high standard of living in conjunction with a relatively clean environment.

It is about time that intelligent and objective people step forward and give the public the whole story concerning nuclear power. The ideologically motivated claptrap that has been used to persuade the American public to drop nuclear power as an energy source is criminal in its misrepresentation of the facts. A future without nuclear power can only be a grim one. The Earth cannot stand another generation of fossil fuel combustion, like the last.

Let's begin with Fukushima and the radioactivity fears that nuclear energy drags around like a boat anchor. These fears have a real basis in fact of course. Radioactivity is invisible and insidious. However, one of the beautiful things about nuclear power and radioactivity is that Geiger counters are cheap. It is extremely difficult in the 21st century, if not impossible to hide problems, like radioactivity leaks.

Some have pointed to Chernobyl as hastening the end for the Soviet Union, because the USSR's reputation was deeply damaged by the nuclear accident. This can be partly attributed to the USSR lying about the state of affairs at the reactor. Their lies were transparent to the world's Geiger counters and destroyed many trusting national relationships. Unlike other technologies and chemicals like MTBE groundwater pollution that cleaned up California's air only to destroy large portions of the state's water supplies, radiation leaks are SUPER EASY for the public to detect with inexpensive Geiger counters. At Fukushima, like Chernobyl, it is impossible for governments and corporations to cover up what is going on and how bad things really are. These facts about radioactivity should be considered real positives by the public, not negatives.

Additionally, citizens should consider that Fukushima is a near worst-case scenario in Japan, a 9.0 earthquake and an 80-foot tsunami hit the reactors and we have not seen the kind of enormous radiation leaks like what was released at Chernobyl. Also, worthy of consideration is that Fukushima is a very old design from decades ago, if this level of safety from an obsolete architecture does not give people some confidence, it is hard to imagine what will.

Another objection to nuclear power is that nuclear waste disposal techniques are inadequate. This argument is not compelling when other power sources are held to the same standard. Current disposal methods for spent fossil fuels are non-existent. We do not trap the exhaust from fossil fuel combustion and put it into barrels. Instead, we spew the poisonous byproducts into our atmosphere.

The waste products of fission are put into barrels and their whereabouts catalogued. Admittedly, those barrels will be hazardous for many thousands of years. However, the waste products of fossil fuels hang around to affect our environment and weather detrimentally for an unknown period. Additionally, spent nuclear fuel can be used in breeder reactors to further reduce waste, not something that can be done in the case of fossil fuels.

Finding a place to store our barrels of radioactive waste should not be as great a problem as many would have us believe. There are large expanses of desert in the American West contaminated by years of nuclear testing. These areas would be perfect for storing barrels of nuclear waste. The US government set off hundreds of nuclear bombs a mere 65 miles from Las Vegas in the fifties and sixties. Over 100 of these atomic bomb tests were above ground and these blasts were visible for miles around. Stacking some barrels of spent nuclear fuel there seems trivial in comparison. Of course, Nevada should be compensated with seriously discounted electricity, maybe even free electricity, to overcome the NIMBY effect that has so dogged America's quest for energy independence.

The American public has an overwhelming fear of nuclear reactors. Three Mile Island scared many people. The amount of radiation released at Three Mile Island should be put into perspective, though. A de-classified document from the 1990s revealed details of a nuclear experiment that went awry, code named Green Run. In the late 1950s, near Spokane, Washington, nearly 8,000 curies of radiation were released. By contrast, the Three Mile Island incident released barely 40 curies. Forty curies are not good, but in comparison to what occurred over 50 years ago when nobody had a Geiger counter, it is minor. Not to mention the government was actually doing publicly viewable airburst bomb tests for decades after WWII, and these seem to have been dissipated by natural processes.

The Green Run experiment and the legacy of airburst atomic bomb testing in the Nevada desert are illustrative. Thousands, perhaps millions, of curies of radiation released into the air, but the government is able to conceal its errors due to the widespread lack of Geiger counters at the time. In addition, there are no huge cancer spikes in Nevada and Utah as one would expect. Obviously, the environment has some capacity to dissipate radiation. After all, uranium is a natural ore, and many areas on Earth are naturally radioactive to some extent. An oil slick, thousands of square miles wide, could never be swept under the rug by the government, because the environment simply cannot dissipate this type of pollution as easily. Before the days of cheap Geiger counters, hiding radiation leaks was not that hard, but the damage from huge oil spills has always been clear for all to see.

The environment does not effectively assimilate oil. Even though the Gulf of Mexico now appears relatively clean, the millions of barrels of oil spilled there still lurk about in the water damaging the health of its inhabitants. In Prince William Sound, the Exxon Valdez accident was far worse than Three Mile Island. It was painful to watch the footage coming from Alaska's Prince William Sound. The animal suffering was so great, even more so than appeared to be the case in the Gulf. News footage of men wiping off Alaska's rocky beaches with towels would have been laughable, had it not been so tragic.

These petroleum disasters will only recur. The world runs on oil. War after war in the Middle East has horribly fouled the Persian Gulf. Arabian marine life will never be the same. Chernobyl, the worst nuclear reactor accident, has a legacy of nature reserves. Truly, the lack of humanity in the Chernobyl "dead zone" has produced a wealth of wildlife and regeneration of the ecology none would have predicted.

Tankers and pipelines crisscross the globe. Thousands of potential disasters are waiting to happen every day AND are happening, but Geiger counters do not pick up oil spills. Major spills are hard to cover up, but continuous minor spillage here and there takes its toll silently. The risks of petroleum cannot be justified when compared to the risks of fission.

The analogy of an urban sewer system is useful when considering the nuclear power situation. The lack of fossil fuel waste disposal condemns us to sit in and breathe our own excrement. With nuclear fission, we can at least put our waste into a septic tank. The nuclear waste comparison to fossil fuel waste clearly demonstrates that fossil fuels are far more toxic, due to the difficulty in containing the waste. What is the half-life of fossil fuel waste?

The United States is demographically and geographically well suited to exploit fission. We still have empty tracts of seismically stable land. A nuclear reactor, a thousand miles or more away, could service San Francisco or Los Angeles or New York. Those same irradiated deserts that played host to underground nuclear bomb tests could be put to the far more beneficial use of generating electricity. The whole of the continental United States might eventually be serviced from a few central locations. Energy production is a national security issue as great as any other, especially since we seem to be heavily involved in the wars and unrest in oil producing regions due to our dependence on foreign oil.

The generation of power for the country is too important to be put in the hands of for profit companies. The potential for profit driving the course of energy generation in this country is too great. Hydrogen power and fuel cell technologies are touted as viable solutions, but again when examined closely, profiteering is revealed. Individuals and corporations with a stake in building a hydrogen-based economy are clearly funding studies that suggest that hydrogen fuel cells can save us from dependence on fossil fuels. These fuel cells are often billed as producing nothing but innocuous water vapor. Every scientist knows that water vapor is a greenhouse gas AND will cause climate change. Pumping industrial amounts of water vapor into the atmosphere cannot help, but change the climate. Hydrogen is driven by the profit hungry and does not make sense.

All of the nuclear plants should be nationalized and run as public utilities in the national interest. The cost of choosing, designing, and building these locations will be astronomical. That is why environmentalists need to rally behind nuclear energy. Nuclear energy does not suffer from the limitations of weather nor does it produce significant climate changing emissions and is a proven industrial strength energy generator. The changing climate demands real alternatives now, not later. Many environmentalists preach conservation. Through conservation, they say, we can reduce emissions, but that is simply not enough.

Environmentalists are ignoring future demand for electrical power that will outstrip conservation savings. For example, if more cities build rail mass transit systems, this could create a new and very large demand for electrical power, since many of these light rail and subway systems are electric. Trains, especially bullet trains, will likely be using superconductivity or wireless power transmission technology and will use enormous amounts of power.

America needs to prepare her infrastructure for the electric car as well. The electric car will move transportation to a mostly electric model. That means later as we build other alternative energy production, we can simply switch out the nuclear backend generation as alternative sources come on line. As other alternatives become more viable or fusion is perfected, we will already have the infrastructure to support a mostly electric transportation model. This makes our infrastructure modular, because we will not have to switch out our transportation infrastructure as our energy generation capabilities evolve. We will just plug in the new electrical generation sources into the backend and our infrastructure just keeps humming along. Right now, we are too dependent on fossil fuels for all manner of industrial and transportation infrastructure.

Current hybrid technologies involve lots of exotic and heavy metals making their green claims somewhat suspect. A better solution would be hybrids with small gasoline engines for around town and electric motors that could be powered on the interstates via wireless power transmission or direct connections embedded in the road rather than carrying batteries. This eliminates the pollution intensive batteries from the equation and allows an electric car to have a much larger range over an electrified interstate system. The electric car's future drain on the power grid is rarely factored into the conservation equations. Huge amounts of electricity will be required for that transition and nuclear fission can provide the juice.

Some studies have shown that a plug-in all electric car will actually generate more carbon emissions than the current internal combustion model using current power generation technologies. This is because the energy has to be created offsite and then transported to the vehicle. Creation of the power within the vehicle by burning gasoline is far more efficient. Because less energy is used to travel a given distance in a gasoline automobile, less pollution is created. Unless the electricity is generated cleanly, the electric car can solve nothing. Small gasoline powered hybrids in town with the ability to couple to an electrified interstate system can bring about a practical future based on fission generated electricity.

Lack of pragmatic reform from the environmental activists has painted our country into a corner. America continued burning cheap oil all throughout the last decade of the 20th century. Oil was so cheap. Two-thirds of Americans opposed a tax on a gallon of gas. It was easy to talk about saving the environment, but if it makes gas prices go up, then Americans could not stomach it. Throughout most of its history, the environmental establishment has focused on what industry and people cannot do, rather than what it can and this has made Americans look at environmentalists as job killers.

We need immediate solutions more than ever. Alternate energy sources are subject to the vagaries of weather and still have a ways to go before they can replace current electrical generation methods. The generation of industrial amounts of electrical power on demand is a tall order. Excess electricity generated on especially sunny or windy days cannot be stored. When there is no wind or sun, then electricity must be generated by oil or natural gas. Solar, tidal, wind and geo-thermal technologies are worth pursuing, but pouring the lion share of our precious financial resources into these technologies is not practical. Such financial expenditures are more about lining the pockets of opportunistic profiteers with government connections, than actually building a new and practical energy generation infrastructure.

Nuclear fission is the lesser of two evils, but certainly the lesser. Precisely because it is not perfect, means that environmentalists must get involved in the production of energy by fission. Progressives will advocate the government nationalization of all nuclear generating facilities to be operated as national public utilities. The lessons of Enron's manipulation of energy generation to boost profits, demonstrates the need to nationalize. This issue is too important to be left in the hands of private industry. Environmentalists must accept the need for nuclear fission and buy in to an agenda for its development. Environmentalists have a role, as government watchdogs, to make sure the bureaucrats do not cut corners at the expense of the environment and safety.

The government currently allows civilian reactors to use only low-grade nuclear fuel because of national security concerns. This creates far more waste than necessary. Nationalization should ease national security concerns and allow the reactors to burn high grade, 99% pure fuel, as the military does. This would decrease the amount of waste created significantly, especially when coupled with a return to using breeder reactors to process some nuclear waste back into fuel. Americans should also realize that military reactors are widely used within our borders. Americans just do not know due to the lack of transparency.

We get additional synergies as well from a clear and focused build out of nuclear generated electricity generation. Research for the development of alternate energy sources could be carried out at the nuclear power plants, making them the sites of national energy laboratories too. Fission is not the final answer, of course, and therefore we can continue to pursue other energy sources. We will continue to chase the elusive goal of controlled fusion. Fusion is the ultimate answer, perhaps, but the use of thorium in future fission processes may also make fission waste easier to deal with.

How ever things evolve in the future, it starts with embracing fission technology as it stands. Our world, as we know it, cannot survive another twenty years of fossil fuel combustion like the last.

In conclusion, readers should consider what a game changer this policy position is. America is painted into a corner. Current trends do not bode well for us. If we continue to import so much energy into the country, other financial expenditures must suffer more than they already do. Finally, imagine America as an energy exporter! Energy would no longer be a source of red ink, but a source of black ink, revenue, in the balance of trade!

What to Do About Water as the Climate Changes

These specific policy positions in the progressive agenda are inter-connected, and it does not do for some pieces to be tossed while others are embraced. The previous section was an all out push for growing our nuclear power energy generation. For all the aforementioned reasons, nuclear power is a good idea, but here is another: its implementation should bring more juice into the electrical grid for problem solving. We can use that extra juice to help bring a solution to our growing water problems.

Any doubts Americans have about the state of water quality in America should simply consider how much bottled water they are drinking. Only those that cannot afford anything else drink tap water regularly in America. Of course, perception and marketing could be driving this, but our own government has admitted that America's water supply contains trace amounts of many polysyllabic chemicals and drugs. Americans pay taxes for water treatment and safe drinking water, but most Americans do not believe that tap water is safe. Scientific analysis of the state of water quality in America certainly confirms the existence of drug residues in water samples all across America, but that is a problem of our own making, which we may be able to solve.

However, just having water that is treatable will be a problem. Global climate change is playing havoc with our 20th-century water distribution networks of dams and aqueducts. Dams in the West, no longer work as designed, due to the early snowmelts that are now occurring. Even in years where the Sierra and Rockies get the expected amounts of snow pack, early spring rains and warming melts the snow pack much faster than it used to. Water that will be needed in the warm summer months is forced to be released because the dam fills too soon. Instead of a slower melt that allows spring usage to draw down the reservoir to make room for subsequent late spring melting, the fast melts mean the dam fills too fast and cannot be drawn down over time. Additional snowmelt ends up just running over the top, because there is no room. Then in the summer, reservoirs are lower than they otherwise would have been, and there is no late spring melt water to quench the summer and autumn thirst.

There is really only one way to deal with this situation, and that is to build desalinization plants. How many we will need depends on how much climate changes affect the American continent's rainfall patterns. Desalinization plants are very expensive in dollars and energy terms. It takes an enormous amount of energy to desalinate seawater. Nuclear power will allow us to have the necessary energy to run these desalinization plants at some kind of reasonable price.

Desalinization has become the only answer, due to our nation's foolish destruction of its own fresh water supplies. Fresh water has been lost due to the pollution of groundwater by our dependence on polysyllabic chemicals and fossil fuels. MTBEs have destroyed groundwater supplies all over California. These chemicals were meant to help gasoline burn cleaner and, therefore, reduce air pollution. Air pollution has been reduced, but at the expense of groundwater, a fool's bargain. Fracking used to extract natural gas might also reduce air pollution since natural gas burns fairly cleanly, but the groundwater risks created by fracking are enormous.

America's abundant water allowed for irrigation of enormous tracts of arable lands. Water is one of America's great blessings, and we have squandered it and may never enjoy the same abundance, due to climate change. America needs climate change to be mitigated, because one of the pillars of our nation's greatness is our favorable climate. Desalinization plants will allow us to irrigate our farmlands, as climate change could severely reduce American rainfall totals. Also, desalinization plants can allow us to irrigate large areas of the country that we will need to return to their native flora.

Given the long-term advantages that our climate has provided us in geo-politics, preventing large-scale climate change is strongly in our national interest. There are some ways, all of them expensive, to handle this environmental crisis. Controlling the climate is beyond our scientific abilities, but we can seek to ally ourselves with those that have been the great climate moderators of history: plant life. Plants and trees filter and transform the atmosphere, producing oxygen from carbon dioxide and water. The urban heat islands that we have created with our cities will need to be tamped down and trees can help us do this.

A large program dedicated to the replanting of native species in the many different microclimates that make up our nation can help us stabilize the continent's climate. Because normal rainfall patterns will likely be changing, we may need to irrigate new native stands of trees that will take decades to actually have a positive effect on our climate. These huge stands of native plant life will also act as a buffer to pollution that the Asian continent will surely be sending our way.

Additionally, in the arid West, there is a growing salinity problem. Irrigation, repeated fertilizer use, and population growth have put enormous pressure on our agriculture-rich western farmlands. The earliest civilizations in Mesopotamia were based on irrigated farmlands. It was salinity in their soils that brought an end to these civilizations of the Fertile Crescent after centuries of prosperity. We now know these fertile lands to be desert-ified Iraq.

Desalinization plants will allow us to flush the salt out of our groundwater over time. This is a common sense plan as speculative as it sounds. It will cost billions to pull it off, but it will gradually pay dividends and, in the end, preserve America's climate advantage. With so much money necessary to pull this off, citizens will need to be heavily involved to give politicians the will to spend the money and make an investment that will not have any short-term benefits, but will pay huge dividends over time. The use of tax dollars in support of public utilities allows for taking the long view.

Adopting these policies will not only preserve America's climate advantage, but will also act as stimulus. Simultaneous institution of such a comprehensive energy production/climate change initiative will create jobs galore. Such job stimulus packages have historically created jobs and will do so again. The state of our national treasury mandates that the government money we spend from now on, not only creates jobs, but also builds out an infrastructure to serve the nation into the future.

Abortion Compromise

For too long, America's political agenda has been dominated by the abortion debate. There is little doubt that readers of the title on both sides of the argument are currently pulling their hair and gnashing their teeth. Yet they have read nothing of what is to follow. For so many, there is no compromise on this issue. America is based upon compromise and we desperately need one here. All down through our history, we have been strengthened by compromises. Both sides of this debate are driven by passions that eliminate any desire for compromise, but without it, American politics will continue to be broken. As a nation, we must find a sensible common ground.

There is a place, where a large majority can reside, unassailable by extremists on either side. The fiery orators on both sides would have us believe that no such middle ground exists. The abortion debate is tearing the country apart. The middle ground exists, and medical science has provided some guidance, but the debate still seems frozen in the seventies. Unfortunately, in America, science is often subject to political spin, as we have seen in the climate debate. As in all things, we need to be guided by science as well as our personal morals.

Legislatively, we have not acknowledged medical science's new facts and realities since the time of the Roe vs. Wade decision. More and more, medical science has demonstrated that the fetus has quite a bit of brain function much earlier than had been previously believed. The images of late-term abortions that medical science can now produce are a powerful argument to revisit the implementation of abortion rights in America. The more medical science has trained its instruments on the abortion procedure, the more the humanity-based objections to unlimited abortion rights gain weight.

Many would agree that the implementation of Roe vs. Wade has been so extreme that it drove the opponents out into streets. A more even-handed implementation of abortion rights would have had its critics, but likely far fewer. The radical approach to abortion rights that was created in the seventies, directly laid the foundation for a groundswell of opposition to abortion. Political opinion will ride a wildly swinging pendulum too often quashing considered arguments. The implementation of Roe vs. Wade is a perfect example of this phenomenon. For example, how can logical adults justify the undermining of parental rights by the state that Roe vs. Wade brought to Main Street America? The fact that under-age girls can get an abortion without even having to tell her parents is a direct attack on parental rights.

At the time, there were some emotional arguments to the contrary, but a certain amount of demonizing of men convinced policymakers that this was the correct implementation of Roe vs. Wade. Rape and forced incest were seen as the reasons for this exception to minors and medical procedures. A less passionate and more reasoned examination of this position would seem to allow such male perpetrators to escape more easily, since there is no obvious pregnancy to cover up in today's world. At the time though, many men felt that women had the right to make the call on this law and many men felt that women were speaking with a unified voice on the matter. In the 21st century, it is clear that women are as divided as men are, now that we have seen the defeat of the Equal Rights Amendment due a lack of female support and with many Christian women now openly opposing abortion of any kind.

Without question, women deserve the right to perform this act of self-determination: ending an unwanted pregnancy. Nonetheless, this wide-open implementation of Roe vs. Wade led directly to an assembly line of publicly funded abortions for underage girls. This energized opposition, mostly religious, to a women's right to an abortion. This is a horrible consequence of the Roe vs. Wade implementation. The complete and unlimited right to abortion to any female, at any time, regardless of age, was a direct attack on the nuclear family by our own government. Of course, there was a backlash to this power grab by government.

A minor girl cannot get a tattoo, but getting an abortion is allowed by the Roe vs. Wade implementation, which defies common sense. Such an implementation is especially offensive to those families with religious objections to abortion, because the law stripped them of their ability to counsel and parent their minor daughters. Allowing children to get abortions without parental consent is one of the most controversial aspects of the implementation of abortion rights in this country.

In the previously male-dominated world of yesterday, if it had been possible for a man to have had his livelihood interrupted by an event similar to pregnancy, there would have been little question that a man would have had the right to defend his right to self-determination. The actual world of yesteryear though led to an oppressive ban on all abortions that caused many tragic consequences for women. The history that led up to Roe vs. Wade, makes it understandable that such a radical implementation would be forced through when the opportunity presented itself. That opportunity presented itself when the Supreme Court decision on Roe vs. Wade was handed down. That decision was found to be onerous to many and it showed how the Supreme Court could be used for political end. As a direct result of their decision, the Supreme Court itself has become heavily politicized.

The outrage over the way the Supreme Court was able to "lord" over the entire nation and force through such a controversial decision as Roe vs. Wade, has had tremendous consequences. The Republican ascendancy in the 21st century is largely based upon its embrace of the "pro-life" agenda. The pro-life litmus test skewed American politics, and it became unbalanced. Politicians that had no business being elected were able to garner support solely upon abortion opposition, no matter how offensive their other political views may have been. The disastrous leadership that drove the American economy into the ditch at the beginning of the 21st century was able to be elected and be re-elected in 2004, almost solely upon their ability to hold the support of evangelical Christians opposed to abortion.

As a country, getting this issue behind us seems an absolute necessity. Abortion debates color every issue, and this cannot continue. We desperately need to analyze issues and vote for politicians that have positions across the board that are considered and supportable. As long as the #1 deciding factor on who to support is driven by this one factor (supports abortion or opposes abortion), we will not be able to tackle other issues and come to a public policy consensus that leads us into the future. We need to be able to debate the nuances of many issues and to strike a course based on facts and considered opinions, because it is the only chance to get out of the hole we have dug ourselves. Abortion has nothing to do with whether to invade another country, but if all a politician has to do is oppose abortion to garner a large percentage of public support for any policy, then we are in a lot of trouble.

Abortion rights advocates hopefully can be brought to the table. There needs to be a realization and acceptance that there are strong moral and humanitarian objections to unlimited abortion held by many reasonable people. Americans must embrace some compromises on this issue. Tyrannical laws are a direct result of the loss of "people power" and too much power centralized in the federal branch. A middle ground exists and it is here at the broad center that Americans should be able to coalesce, defusing the abortion issue and preventing the further corruption of American political decisions by this single-issue war.

So here it is, the compromise decision that should be able to stake out a middle ground that a majority of Americans can gravitate to, abandoning the demagogues on both sides and their extremist supporters...

Wait, wait...no gnashing of teeth and hair pulling!

At the federal level, an adult woman's right to unlimited abortion should only extend out 6 months or 24 weeks. After all, the right to privacy bumps up against practical reality, since the pregnancy is quite obvious by this point. In addition, science has demonstrated that the fetus can be born AND survive. This then allows the people of each of the states to modify their abortion access as they see fit after this cut-off date. If voters in California want to continue to allow minor abortions without parental consent and later into pregnancy, then they should have that right. If Texas wants to limit minor abortions to parental consent as long as it was coupled with some path for a minor to petition (the court for emancipation), then that should be allowed as well. This frames the issue within a broad Constitutional framework that allows some local legal latitude at the state level.

Localizing a moral issue to the state level allows for some regional variation. This flexibility allows for some slack in the law, acknowledging that there are serious moral and religious objections to unlimited abortions. If abortion rights advocates, continue to hold that the current implementation is all there is, then we will continue to have our government's operation held hostage to this debate.

Sometimes we just have to compromise and accept a solution that can work for the long-term, because there is just too much disagreement for a central solution to be imposed upon all. Power to the People, above all, will require tolerance. Freedom is just messy, and tolerance is an absolute must.

Ending Prohibition

Prohibition nearly destroyed our country once before, and it is certainly dragging us down again. For generations now, we have reversed the individual freedom gains that the permissive society delivered in the wake of the sixties. The intended purpose of this strong reversal, this War on Drugs, is to increase public safety. However, public safety has not increased, in fact, in some areas public safety has eroded in ways directly related to the illegality of certain substances. We have very little positive to show for the hundreds of billions of dollars that we have spent fighting the War on Drugs and bringing back a more authoritarian society. The costs to personal liberty have been staggering. We have eliminated many constitutional protections in our rabid pursuit of this alleged War on Drugs.

Criminalizing personal behavior destroys the free society. The earlier Prohibition on alcohol demonstrated this fairly clearly, as criminalizing the victim-less behaviors of otherwise productive citizens financed crime and was destructive to law and order in general. In the final analysis, alcohol prohibition was a miserable failure creating many more negative effects in society than alcohol abuse ever did. Worth noting here, is the fact that the original Prohibition, alcohol prohibition, required an amendment to the Constitution and when Prohibition was finally ended, the Constitution was amended again. For some reason our government decided it no longer had to follow these constitutional protocols in the War on Drugs.

Certain basic practical realities must be adhered to in a free society. One of those pragmatic realities is that criminalizing normal human behavior destroys freedom. The altering of one's mood chemically is as old as human history. Most of the so-called recreational drugs have a molecular structure similar to naturally occurring substances in the human body. The drugs have a molecular make-up that allows them to bond to specific receptors in the brain, mimicking the effects of chemicals normally manufactured by the body in connection with certain emotions. Chemically altering ones mental state is a normal human behavior.

Humans are electrochemical engines. The makers of the many anti-depressants on the market have proven this fact over and over. For some odd reason, the government has allowed these anti-depressant drugs to be used on our populace, while prohibiting other psychoactive drugs with much longer track records of use, such as marijuana. Anti-depressants have even been allowed to be given to our children, sometimes with suicidal results. Why do government and medical experts claim to be able to read the minds and emotional states of free individuals and to mandate what molecule bonds in a satisfactory manner to an individual's brain receptors?

The drive to alter mental states is a strong one. With the government cracking down even harder on mainstream recreational drugs, people have begun to turn to all kinds of alternatives. Prescription drugs are all the rage. Even sniffing paint and other volatile chemicals, known as huffing, is still practiced despite the well-known immediate detrimental effects to brain cells. The fact is that huffing is more destructive to its practitioners than just about any of the hard drugs. There is talk of making spray paint a controlled substance, instead of rolling back the draconian drug laws in an effort to reduce societal and individual harm. This is because we seem to have only one solution, illegality and can see no other.

As a practical matter, not every naturally occurring chemical that can alter a person's mood can or should be made illegal. It is not widely known, but the seeds of some common garden plants contain a substance very similar to LSD. Will we make every cottage garden illegal? The current American tendency is to regulate and come up with laws making each naturally occurring plant molecule illegal. Many legislators call for laws against these different plants, but it is terribly impractical. Chemists are always out to copy plant molecules in such a way as to make a synthetic version of some naturally occurring drug to avoid the law, anyway.

Manufacturing drugs obviously requires government oversight and control in the name of public safety. However, our legislatures are spending so much time researching and writing bills to make these chemicals illegal and then creating enforcement regimes that we often get little other law-making done. Which some would argue are exactly the consequences those making money from this prohibition want.

Why do Americans believe that our government is responsible and we should allow it to imprison people for using this chemical or that one? The government has a horrible record in the drug arena. The old alcohol prohibition or the anti-depressant caused suicides in teenagers are perfect examples of the government's track record, but there are others. The federal government and the FDA actually blocked release of a safer cigarette. In the eighties, the tobacco industry had developed a safer, smokeless cigarette. Essentially, the safer cigarette was a plastic tube that delivered the nicotine without the tar and other carcinogens. The FDA labeled it a drug delivery system and prevented it from coming to market. Of course, it was a drug delivery system, but so is the standard paper cigarette.

Despite much shouting to the contrary, the tobacco industry is not quite as evil as the tax-hungry politicians have made them out to be. Preventing the tobacco companies from bringing their safer cigarette to market has preserved thirty years of tax revenue to state, local, and federal government through their sin taxes. The reality is that the government bears a huge responsibility for continuing lung cancer and emphysema deaths that have occurred over the last thirty years. The government's main mission should be the well-being of its citizenry without significantly curtailing personal freedom, and it has failed on both fronts.

Additionally, we must consider relief for our overloaded justice system. We should all be concerned about the fact that we imprison more of our population per capita than any other western nation on Earth. How can we call ourselves the land of the free in light of that statistic? One of the most beneficial consequences of legalization would be the family reunions that would happen all across the country as non-violent drug offenders returned home. Another exciting, beneficial consequence of legalization is taking the money out of the hands of the scum balls and lowlifes of this earth. Serious consideration of this idea sends shivers down the spine of every one of these horrific leeches on humanity.

This country should not forget the monetary consequences of this war, either. A trillion dollars of controlled substances may be hitting our streets every year after we have already spent at least that amount to prevent it. We really do not know how much is actually hitting the street unmonitored and untaxed. The free market has been speaking loudly on this issue for some time now. Throughout history, America has obeyed the free market most of the time. When we have tried to defy the market, we have often made the situation worse. One reason America cannot balance her budget relates directly to this trillion dollar black market economy that goes unaccounted, unregulated, and, above all, untaxed.

If we want to have a balanced budget, reduce prison overcrowding, and take the pressure off the police force so it can tackle real crimes against the public order, we must begin to legalize, starting with marijuana. Death from an overdose of marijuana continues to be unproven, while alcohol poisoning is a well known cause of death in the medical literature. Of course, in the current climate, investigating the toxic effects of marijuana requires better data than the black market can supply. In this regard, Prohibition makes us less safe.

Many question how drug legalization could work, but there is a simple roadmap. Legalization should start with marijuana, which is the obvious choice, because prison populations are swollen with inmates arrested for mere possession of marijuana and the drug is relatively benign. Additionally, the drug is a plant and requires very limited processing beyond picking and drying. Many unexpected quarters of America may actually come to strongly support this route to ending Prohibition, because it could benefit some of the big corporations and create jobs.

The cigarette companies would have another substance to use in their cigarette factories. Small farmers dependent upon shrinking demand for tobacco crops could now grow marijuana for domestic consumption. Processing of the plant will be kept to a minimum to prevent the manufacture of ever more powerful versions distilled by pharmaceutical processes.

This is how drug legalization can work. Naturally occurring substances within plants are going to eventually become legal over the course of a progressive drug policy. If marijuana legalization is successful, coca leaves and perhaps even opium could be added to the list of frowned upon, but tolerated, drugs. It would be the unprocessed plant material that would be made legal, not the industrially refined versions of coca, crack cocaine and opium's refined brethren, morphine and heroin.

This approach causes the least harm to society by limiting prison populations, reducing the exchange of deadly anonymous white powders and generating some tax revenue, too. Economically, the benefits of plant-based legalization are dramatic for the American farmer. By allowing farmers to grow these high profit crops, we can begin to reduce the subsidies that have become little more than corporate welfare for agribusiness.

Finally, the old Prohibition actually caused more children to get involved in alcohol, because of the illegality hampered real regulation. When alcohol became legal again, it became easier to regulate its distribution and prevent minors from easily getting access to alcohol Similarly, ending our current prohibition could help prevent drug use in children by limiting access through legalization and regulation. More importantly, we do not know why America, with five percent of the population of the world, consumes over fifty percent of the world's cocaine production. Legalization will finally begin to give us the data we need to understand why the American populace seems so susceptible to this chemical scourge. Make no mistake this is a compromise solution to mitigate societal harm. As a people, we still need to think about and understand why we are the global center of drug abuse in the world.

Is It About Civil Unions or Marriage?

Progressives should realize that all this fuss about gay marriage is really missing the point. Once upon a time, protecting marriage as an institution had a much higher purpose in society. It had to do with the fact that a given culture does not go on without future generations. Each society and nation's future is almost completely based upon their fertility and not their military power, especially when one takes the long view. In fact, historically, one can look at many supposedly successful conquests that were actually demographically nullified within a few generations; Alexander the Great and Genghis Khan are two perfect examples. History may even look back on America's passion for Manifest Destiny and the Mexican-American War in this light some day

Unfortunately, in our society, marriage no longer serves America's ultimate purpose of continuation. DINKs (Dual Income, No Kids) have become the norm, and the gay population is heavily represented here—as one might expect. This should be the heart of the debate, not whether gay people can get married, but rather that marriage now fails us as a positive social force for the future. Many heterosexuals enter into marriage with only hedonistic goals. They imagine a life of continuous sex and lower tax brackets without the burdens of children, just as many homosexual couples are dreaming of similarly burden-less lives.

Who will pay these people's Social Security and Medicare or fight their wars, and who will otherwise provide society with the new wave of movers and shakers that the future will always demand? It will be those that have children, and bear the resulting burdens of child rearing. Hedonism is truly a short-term lifestyle, which hands down very little to future generations. The financial and time burdens are enormous to raise children to a productive adulthood. As a society, we need to value families and children, because they are the future.

There should be greater tax breaks for children's breadwinners. Parents should not have to buy health insurance for their child. Society has a huge interest in healthy children. All honest studies of the matter demonstrate the positive economic impact of taking care of the health of children in a society. We could even extend the argument to the fact that the caregivers of children are making sacrifices in the name of posterity and should be extended health insurance.

Because the specific act of marriage no longer provides the enormous societal benefits that it used to and since we are in the search for more tax revenues, we should end the tax break for getting married. This tax break only makes sense when society expected the married couple to then help bring in the new generation, by either birth or adoption. This tax break works in a society where one of the purposes for getting married is to start a family, but not so well where marriage no longer guarantees children. Children exist in a shrinking portion of marriages, and to have the tax code support hedonism is self-defeating. America should pump up the deductions for dependents—be they children or adult parents. Either way, the support of dependents by their families is a key portion of the social safety net of the nation. We should reward it, not ignore it.

Until the tax code is reformed on this issue, discussions on gay marriage are premature and are just going to cost the nation tax revenues as these couples then start stumping for tax breaks like their heterosexual counterparts. We have already been belabored with discussions of extending dependent status to pets in the tax code during the last few years. That this received any traction at all showed a certain social disconnect related to the future's need for children. Gay people have some biologic hurdles to providing children for the future that most heterosexuals are not facing, no doubt. If the gay population wants to get married, then they should be vocal and more up front on childhood adoption and support of adult parent issues.

Why do we not see this type of fervor in pursuit of adoption rights in the gay community? There are plenty of religious and moral zealots that consistently oppose gay adoption, just as they oppose gay marriage. Progressives will see the strong need to involve the gay population in the social support network and reject self-righteous moralizing. If gays brought a passion to the issue of supporting society's future, then the gay adoption opponents would be forced to adopt all the orphans in the nation before their voices had any credibility. Some would argue that the reason gays do not push the issue more is because there is a heavy streak of selfishness in this constituency, but progressives will seek to invigorate the social consciousness of this constituency as part of any support for gay marriage.

Progressives also recognize that gays should not talk of marriage in terms of civil rights, portraying it in the same light as the fight that people of color fought in the last century. This only reinforces the view of narrow-minded selfishness that some accuse this community of, because people of color in this nation were clearly economically deprived for many decades due to discrimination. The facts were all there for people to see in the slums and barrios, where people of color were segregated. In contrast, the gay population is one of the most financially well-off constituencies in this nation as determined by financial survey after survey. Progressives should steer away from attempts to portray the fight for gay marriage as a civil rights battle, because it truly diminishes the sacrifice of all those that suffered the squalor of economic inequality for decades, even centuries, based on nothing more than the color of their skin.

Progressives will need to defuse a growing core of fanatic chauvinists on both sides of this issue. Some gays will deride heterosexuals with a nasty term of scorn, like "breeders". This "breeders" nickname is a hurtful term. To be referred to as a "breeder", implies that the heterosexual is some kind of an animal on a farm. Somehow, the heterosexual is a lesser being for having fulfilled their biological destiny. Despite this derision, the children of "breeders" will provide the tax dollars to pay into the system that supports all that are aged and unable to care for themselves. The hard-core chauvinists that exist on both sides stifle the possibility for progress on the issues involved.

As is often the case in these seemingly intractable issues facing us as a nation, the intractability is in the improper framing of the debate. By seeing marriage as a right AND a responsibility that requires more than endless sex with your monogamous partner of choice, while wearing a ring to proclaim your love, the issue becomes much clearer. Clearly, DINKs and their hedonistic lifestyles deserve no tax breaks. No greater social purpose is served by giving dependent-less hetero or homosexual couples a lower tax bracket. When seen in terms of society's future, the issue is not so intractable, because we as a society could use the help of gay marriages that support dependents. After all gays represent one of the wealthiest large demographics in America and leveraging it as part of our social support network is a win-win for all.

Progressives will expect gay people to include in their marriage activism the message about the higher purpose of marriage: family, children, and the future of society. This issue is deeper, and it is about family and the future. If gays want this right, then they should be talking about the full depth and breadth of the right and how, by their inclusion, they understand the greater purpose of society and wish to shoulder their load. Rights just aren't candy and ice cream, because there are obligations that go with rights!

If the gay community is ready to step up and embrace all of their rights and duties, then, yes, progressives will loudly proclaim the need for homosexuals to join heterosexuals in America's distributed family support network. Participation in that network would of course bring with it the blessings, privileges and legal protections of marriage or civil union.

Social Security

The balancing of America's budget has been a political hot potato for more than a generation, and Social Security is more than ever a target for that balancing act. Make no mistake about it, Social Security is called Social Security, because it is a socialist program, and FDR would certainly have seen himself as something of a socialist. Let us get that out of the way. Social Security is a socialist program championed by a socialist President. However, Social Security as it exists today is not the pay-as-you-go old age pension for retired workers envisioned by Franklin Delano Roosevelt. Americans should understand that Social Security as we see it today is not FDR's vision, but it is rather a Republican vision and reluctant execution of a popular socialist program they could not kill outright.

In 1980, Ronald Reagan was elected on promises to cut government overspending. His budget director, David Stockman, was center stage almost immediately. Seemingly, every day, Stockman was under fire for recommending another program be cut. To a political animal like Ronald Reagan, it was clear that Americans wanted to pay less for government, but they did not necessarily wish to cut any programs. Reagan and his brain trust made the politically astute decision to fire David Stockman, because the American people only wanted lower taxes. When Reagan actually tried to do what he said he was going to do, most people balked at their government program being cut. Progressives must accept that the dead body that lies at our doorstep as many trillions in debt is the responsibility of the people as much as the politicians

A lack of honesty and attention by our citizenry helped create this mountain of debt and that cannot be overemphasized. The progressive agenda cannot and will not succeed without an empowered and engaged populace. We have devoted many chapters to that empowerment, but engagement is just as important. The election in 1980 of Ronald Reagan and the mythology that has grown out of his presidency is illustrative of the lack of attention citizens have paid to what has actually been going on in the American tax code.

This is not to indict the Reagan presidency, but rather the people for not paying attention and not being honest. Reagan and the Congressional Democrats made a deal to save Social Security. Reagan hired none other than Alan Greenspan, before he became head of the Federal Reserve, to heavily rework the Social Security program. This huge rework of Social Security seems to have been forgotten in today's debt debates.

Reagan's cutting of the tax rates in the United States has entered into American mythology. To the unobservant, it appeared that Reagan's budget and tax code rework was a tax break. However, when one looks more closely at what the Reagan administration did in the 1980s, the tax break is far less than it has been historically trumpeted as. Normal income tax brackets were standardized and overall income taxes were lower, that is true. Largely unreported was that Social Security taxes were raised significantly at the same time. This allowed the government to then have more tax revenues to spend by looting the Social Security Trust Fund. Reagan's alleged tax cuts actually confirmed Keynesian economic ideas, when the greater government spending led to an economic boom.

Social Security had been a pay as you go program, but under the Greenspan rework of the tax code, Social Security began collecting more taxes than it needed to meet its obligations. The standard income taxes did go down under Reagan, but this served as a massive tax cut for the rich and a pittance for the middle class and poor due to the large increase in Social Security taxes. To understand how the Reagan era tax cuts heavily favored the rich and well off, we have to look at the numbers.

The Greenspan plan has been devastatingly effective in shifting the burden of taxation onto working people. The numbers are damning. The progressive American citizen will need to put some brain cells online to understand the numbers, hence the need for real engagement. In the case of a family of four, with an income of, say, $80,000, the difference in taxes paid by one family of four versus another family of four can differ by as much as a factor of ten, sometimes even more. The huge difference is based upon how a family "earns" their money. If the family happens to be part of a larger, wealthier family, or one of the members is a trust fund baby, the income from a modest trust fund generating dividends and long-term capital gains would pay less than $1,000 in taxes on $80,000 of income. On the other hand, the federal tax bill for a working family with the same income and not enough deductions to open any other schedules would be over $12,000, half of which would be going to the Social Security tax. An additional $6,000 would be paid by their employers to yield a stunning $18,000.00 in revenues for the central government from the working family versus a mere $1,000.00 from the trust fund family!

The trust fund family uses the roads, and their children attend the schools, yet they pay less than a tenth in taxes of the working family. Astonishingly even the upper middle class wage earner is discriminated against, for those working families that make more than $100,000 from one wage earner, the income over the 100K mark will not be subject Social Security taxes. However, for the two wage earner family where they average together well over $100K of income, they continue to pay into to Social Security because neither earner reaches the cut-off threshold. In fact, it can take upwards of $200,000 of income in the two wage earner family before their income is no longer subject to the Social Security tax. This is the true legacy of the Reagan tax reform. A disproportionate amount of the tax burden was shifted to the wage earners with the promise that the extra tax dollars being collected would be saved in a Social Security Trust Fund.

Progressives recognize that Social Security tax dollars are owed to the people, and mostly to the working class people. The Reagan reform should have set Social Security to pay for itself, but we are now hearing that it will go bankrupt. Our elected leaders have been removing the money from the Social Security Trust Fund for many years now. That money has been allegedly invested in special government bonds that are paying rates of around 4% on the principal. The Social Security Trust Fund is actually empty, and there is a big fat IOU sitting in that account. The people hold an IOU for trillions that the American government is beginning to seem a little wobbly about paying back. This is the true reason that Standard and Poor's and the Chinese downgraded American debt. The American government has already begun to default on some of its very real debt obligations in the eyes of those looking in from the outside.

There continues to be a huge revenue stream from Social Security taxes, even if that does not cover 100% of outgoing expenses. The Clinton budget surpluses were actually based upon the enormous surplus that the Social Security system was running under. Progressives understand the American citizen has paid for a secure, supportive social safety net. Progressives must also understand that it will cost money—trillions, in fact, to pull it off. Progressively restoring American greatness will require an investment in our people. Investing in our people will pay dividends, but there is no way for us honestly to quantify that dividend amount. No question, it may require some tax increases at the higher income levels, but over the long term, it is better for everyone.

Americans want these entitlement programs to go on despite the financial obstacles. Americans want a social safety net. Working Americans are owed these dollars. Americans want unemployment and disability insurance, along with Social Security and Medicare. Nonetheless, America's social programs need to be restructured, and built-in cost of living adjustments need to be recalculated, if we are to create anything sustainable. Reform of the existing programs will not be enough, but it will help, of course.

The definition of the true social safety net we as a society want to provide needs to be clearly defined. To salvage Medicare and Social Security as pillars of the American social safety net, they may need to become one pay as you go program. As part of that merger, a simple expansion of Medicare for everyone will create a true social safety net that makes sure Americans have access to healthcare and support in disability and old age. Initial funding will come from all of the IOUs our government owes the people. This is how it must be. America's greatness is locked up in her people and unless we invest in our people, there can be no Progressive Restoration.

Healthcare Reform

Ever since the days of Medicare, government-run and subsidized healthcare has been demonized. When Medicare was first proposed, it was condemned as socialism that would bring an end to the American way of life. Of course, it was socialism and Americans like their socialism as long as it is not called socialism. On this issue, we need to grow up as a people and accept the fact socialism is a part of every society. How much socialism in a given social system is just a matter of degree. The reality is that for generations now the government-run system of Medicare has been relatively successful.

It would be disingenuous not to admit that less than 20 years after its inception in 1965, the program had to be reconfigured to raise the taxes that paid for it. In addition, program costs since that rejiggering in 1982 have increased at a staggering rate. Nonetheless, it has been a success, insofar that the recipients are happy and Americans in general continue to support it. Medicare is a costly program to be honest, but one gets what one pays for in America.

In 2008, the upheaval in American politics that led to the election of Barack Obama and the Democratic majorities that swept into the legislative branches of government sent the pundits to their chalkboards. Their analysis concluded that the electoral swing was driven to some extent by the belief among the people that some kind of universal healthcare was very necessary. Americans knew the Republicans were not going to deliver it. Democrats took this as a mandate for change on the health care front, and they immediately set to work on healthcare reform.

Unfortunately, what the Democrats produced does not look like any kind of real reform, but rather some minor rule changes. Americans probably realized such a program would be costly, but this half-measure costs money without really fixing much. In fact, it seems like Obamacare was created by the medical insurance industry to protect their monopoly.

We as a country spend more of our GDP on healthcare than any other developed nation. We cannot get something for nothing, and Americans understand that. However, despite paying such a premium as a country, we do not have the longest life spans or lowest infant mortality rates. Honestly, there is very little that we can point to as successful in our current health care system, with the exception of insurance company profits.

During the Republican reign at the beginning of this century, the Medicare drug benefit was signed into law. This new Medicare benefit was touted as a huge success. A closer look reveals that the only victory was for drug companies. Within the bill, the government and the people were denied the ability to fight for better prices. The government and the people were denied the option of importing the very same drugs being sold at lower prices in countries all across the world. Why is this? Any way you look at it, the United States people are subsidizing drug prices all across the globe. This alleged reform by Republicans ended up being an industry-written and, therefore, industry-favoring legislation.

The Medicare drug benefit was little more than a repackaging and institutionalizing of the Medigap plans that had been in existence for decades. To get on the Medicare drug benefit, the subscriber had to pay about the same price to get about the same benefit that already existed in private industry supplemental insurance. Of course, the drug companies had no problem with this legislation, because it allowed them to lock the government and the people into this two-tiered pricing system. This is the history of what has masqueraded as healthcare reform in this country for too long. Corporate-written legislation is passed through our legislature under the guise of reform and assistance to the people.

This is why the Democrats' alleged healthcare reform has been rejected by the people. They are fed up with being sold down the river by their own government. The people have no faith that the government can come up with anything new that is not going to feather the nests of the politicians, the corporations, or both. Democrats can howl about how necessary healthcare reform is, but if what was delivered to the people in 2009 is what Democratic healthcare reform will be, then many don't want it. Neither

Republican nor Democrat, nor Liberal nor Conservative can strongly support the new healthcare reform if they are truly seeking to improve the lives of United States citizens.

Democratic healthcare reform has been rejected by the people, not because it was socialism and too costly, as Republicans want to say, but for very specific reasons that go unmentioned by the right. The bill mandated that everyone had to buy health insurance to spread risk creating a complete pool for American insurers, but it did not provide a public option for this mandate. What a boon to the insurance companies! They now had a captive clientele. To try to make this more palatable, there are subsidies to those that could not afford the healthcare insurance. This is just more public money into the coffers of insurance companies and makes poor Americans feel like beggars with such subsidies. There is already a huge amount of public money in the healthcare system, and any more public money in the system should directly fund a public system, otherwise it is too costly. Without the efficient example of Medicare and a public option, private insurance companies will just fleece the people and keep their profit margins very healthy.

Strangely, Republicans feel it is OK for the government to subsidize insurance premiums in the private sector, but actually to administrate a taxpayer insurance company is unacceptable. Most Americans are fed up with sending money to the private sector, like TARP, and expecting that this money will be used to benefit the society as a whole. Medicare runs on about as low an administrative overhead as possible, while the private sector is running at many times that overhead. It is no wonder private industry would not want to compete with the public option, because Medicare has proven public funded healthcare can be run efficiently. Somehow, the horribly inefficient government is outperforming the private sector. The private sector claims to be more efficient than government, but we are learning as a nation that the private sector tends to send all their alleged efficiency savings to executive bonuses.

Another horrible and unacceptable aspect of the Democratic healthcare reform is the tax on so-called Cadillac plans, which meant that anyone that had traded salary for better health insurance was going to get the shaft. Taxing families that already have given up some salary for better health insurance is not going to get their support.

Self-employed individuals that try to navigate the health insurance maze themselves become painfully aware of something known as the UCR, the usual and customary rate. Insurance companies negotiate with doctors for a rate that is always some percentage of this UCR, never the full amount. Therefore, the only people that are ever charged this UCR are people that do not have health insurance at all. The self-employed head of household MUST get some form of health insurance to prevent his family from being charged more than everyone else is.

Individuals end up paying for almost all of their family's health insurance costs out of their own pocket due to the large deductibles charged to individuals and their families. Many families are paying thousands of dollars a year in premiums just to avoid paying the UCR. That means they are paying for nothing more than a fee schedule and no other benefit. Unless something catastrophic happens to them or their family, they are a gravy train for a health insurance company. This is where the public option would give everyone the ability to pay less than the UCR, and end the insurance monopoly. Clearly, it makes sense for the government to step in and start imposing a fee schedule on everyone, but an industry-written bill will never go there.

Industry-written legislation extends the medical insurance monopoly rather than breaking it. Americans that now take the risk of not having insurance, sometimes actually make out better in the end, if they are lucky enough to be healthy over a long period. Now even this terrible gamble is removed from the table as an option with mandated coverage. As terrible as it is, no coverage as an option does sometimes pay-off.

Therein lays the problem with private health insurance. It is a for profit enterprise, which sees sick individuals as a hit to the bottom line that must be mitigated. Progressives realize that healthcare should be a public utility that is regulated. When we look at social problems of this nature, we all instinctively understand that the government is the place where such problems can be addressed. Unfortunately, our government is no longer advocating for its own citizens.

Medicare is a costly plan right now. There is no question that as the population ages, it only gets more costly. Medicare was created to address the fact that older Americans could not get affordable health coverage in the 20th century. Being old means they are obviously going to have more health problems than younger individuals would. Therefore, the idea of expanding Medicare to encompass a greater percentage of the population and, therefore, get some spreading of the risk does make sense.

The question of how far to expand it, and to whom, is where the conundrum is. Medicare enjoys the support of Americans now, but that program came from a government that no longer exists. Expansion of Medicare should have been one of the first steps on the road to reforming health insurance, but current moneyed interest groups are writing our legislation and getting politicians to sell it as reform. Obviously, this is costly and hard to pay for, but in the end, a healthier populace serves our society as a whole better.

Right now, our health as a nation is running in the wrong direction. One way to begin to collect real data on the health of our population is to open Medicare to everyone that wishes to join for a set period. Who will jump in? How much will it cost? What are the common health issues plaguing us? We need to collect this data. We can also give an immediate boost to our nation's health by instituting a plan of this nature for a set period. When it would start and its duration would have to be shrouded in secrecy. All day, every day, this nation implements black budget items that are classified and never see the light of day as national security issues. This is clearly a national security issue. An unhealthy populace strikes directly at the heart of our nation's security.

By implementing it as a one-time deal, for a limited duration, we do not lock in a huge budget problem for generations, but we do give a boost to our populace. We do get to collect real data on the state of the uninsured, and even the insured, in this nation and do not create another revenue stream for private industry. This is the first step to real healthcare reform, the collection of data, and the immediate assistance to an ailing citizenry. It is, of course, only a stopgap measure, but it would begin to put into practice some kind of public option to compete against the private sector.

Cost data is very important to collect. In the final analysis, the cost of medical care must be addressed. The costs of drugs and procedures will need to be regulated in some way. If these costs are regulated, then it will be a boost to the profit margins of insurers, who surely will not pass on these savings to the private citizen unless there is a public option. A temporary public option, one that is collecting data to verify industry claims of poverty, is vital.

Somehow, we found trillions to bailout financial entities, even funneling many billions to foreign banks, to prevent losses for investors that took legitimate investing risks that should have cost them money. All that money is public taxpayer money that was printed and shipped to benefit offshore interests. Finding the money to collect the health data and cost data is an investment in our future and ourselves. Those who oppose it are unpatriotic.

We can afford some public option, especially in the current private insurance climate. Hopefully, a temporary public option will make it clear to private insurance industry executives that they must provide affordable healthcare or lose their monopoly and market share altogether. Cost data gleaned from this temporary expansion of Medicare to anyone will allow us to begin coming up with a real plan to regulate costs in healthcare.

Citizens should remember that this problem, like many others was a long time coming and essentially of our own making. Ronald Reagan signed into law in 1986 the Emergency Medical Treatment and Active Labor Act, which required hospitals to provide stabilizing treatment for patients with emergency medical conditions, including childbirth, without first demanding evidence of ability to pay. This unfunded mandate has been putting a social burden on private medical providers for decades.

Today many individuals just wait until they can wait no longer and then show up in the emergency room for service. Law requires these individuals to be treated, but provides no money to pay for it. Logically, that service should not be forced on the hospital without someone paying the cost. Private industry simply passes on the costs of these uncollectible debts from emergency room treatments. Perhaps this is one of the reasons medical costs have skyrocketed. At least in part, government has put a burden on private medical care providers, and as a for profit enterprise, these costs are passed on from the subscribers to the system. These hidden cost burdens rarely enter into the public debate on universal healthcare.

Developed nations all across the world have some universal healthcare, and all have some component that is a public option. These plans also require individuals to get health insurance, but that is in conjunction with a public option or at least heavy regulation of healthcare premiums and provider costs. Universal healthcare systems vary in the extent of government involvement in providing a single payer or public option healthcare delivery system.

In some countries, such as the Great Britain, Spain, Italy, and the Scandinavian countries, the government has a high degree of involvement in the delivery of healthcare. Access is based on residency, not on the purchase of insurance. Other countries have more eclectic delivery systems, based on obligatory health insurance with contributory insurance rates related to salaries or income. Employers and employees also usually fund the plans jointly. Sometimes, the funds are derived from a mixture of insurance premiums and government taxes. Some countries, such as the Netherlands and Switzerland, operate via privately owned, but strongly regulated, private insurers.

All of the aforementioned universal healthcare systems function relatively well. though not always inexpensively. The measure of their success can be measured in life spans, infant mortality, and many other yardsticks of the overall health of a given nation's population. Very few Americans can sit back and claim that healthcare delivery in this nation is not horribly broken and does not need reform given the real health statistics.

The problem is that very few Americans trust the politicians to act in their interest anymore. This means that any reform must somehow bypass the politicians. A way to do this is to institute a temporary public option in Medicare and begin getting real numbers, not speculative numbers, on the cost of such a system. Medicare already exists, and therefore, by simply opening it up in its current form, lobbyists and other special interest groups have a much smaller chance to manipulate things to preserve their own interests or their sponsor's interests.

It may very well be that an expansion of Medicare as is into the healthcare delivery system is the permanent solution that we simply must find the money to fund. Americans should realize that no amount of classified, black budget, security expenditures will protect our nation from age or the scourge of disease. Health of our citizens in this nation is a primary security issue in a very direct way, not in some intangible way. Also, the instituting of an existing public option in the private sector puts real pressure on private industry to get it together and provide an efficient alternative to a public option, if they can really do it. Currently, corporate insurers may not be using their private funding methods in as efficient a fashion as they could. Giving the private insurers a captive client base without setting up a competing public option fails to motivate them adequately and will not deliver the results we need.

Most current, universal healthcare systems were implemented in an attempt to adhere to Article 25 of the Universal Declaration of Human Rights of 1948, a declaration from the United Nations General Assembly. It was signed by almost every country currently operating a universal healthcare system. The U.S. did not ratify the social and economic rights sections, including Article 25's right to health. Americans today are paying the price for not recognizing the real necessity of basic healthcare. Healthcare should truly be a right. It is a life and death issue and one that cannot be left to private industry's for profit delivery system.

A publicly funded healthcare option is not the job killer that Republicans claim it to be. As General Motors discovered in Canada, it was actually better for the bottom line to pay a bit more taxes and have healthcare be a part of the social safety net. The lack of health care insurance being a part of that safety net is a drag on business. Without healthcare reform, individuals have problems starting their own businesses and creating the ownership society envisioned by the business friendly politicians that oppose the reform. An individual with a family is virtually forced to work for a large corporation to absorb the healthcare costs, because the individual is discriminated against in the current system. Without question, the American healthcare system is stifling economic growth and must be fixed.

Taxes and Revenues

Looking at our debt problems, one can be excused for believing that cutting spending is the only answer. However, this enthusiasm for austerity should be kept in the context that there have been tax cut upon tax cut for the upper tax brackets leading up to our current budgetary woes. Instead of bringing the promised economic boom, we stand upon the edge of a fiscal abyss. Obviously, the very first thing to do is end the Bush tax cuts for the rich. These tax cuts have quite clearly led to oceans of red ink without any discernible assistance in job creation.

Cut, cut, cut the taxes is all we hear, but we have been hearing it for over 20 years now. We have spent more than a generation feeding the rich all the tax cuts they can handle and either borrowing the money or reducing social programs to pay for it. By now, it is clear this is not effective or responsible tax policy given our current monetary situation. We do not have strong economic growth or job creation, but we have mountains of debt.

Despite our economic straits, we must continue to spend for our future. We are still the largest economy in the world and with that the largest government budget in the world. Many understand that a huge portion of the budget resides in Social Security, Medicare and military spending. The truly unfortunate thing that some Americans are waking up to is that the over collection of tax revenue that was supposed to be put in a trust to pay for Social Security in the future has been pirated and used for tax cuts for the rich. Were the Social Security Trust Fund packed with the cash that has been over collected in the previous 30 years, our budgetary crisis would not be a crisis.

Nonetheless, we must continue to invest in ourselves and in our country. We can no longer afford to feed the rich tax cuts that never trickle down or build bombs for the military that never create infrastructure. Before the day of reckoning comes, we must force our government to invest in infrastructure and social support, because these are the budget items that can pay dividends in the future.

Dividends that can be game changers are what we need. Bombs and tax cuts for wealthy people that do not need them do nothing for this nation economically. Investment in roads, healthcare, education, telecommunications, technology and a host of other infrastructure-related capital expenses can yield dividends that are impossible to calculate ahead of time. Investments like this in the past brought forth the intangibles that made America the super power of the 20th century.

American citizens will have to force that type of investment today though, because politicians do not have the will to resist their wealthy and corporate masters. Any doubts we had of this should have been cleared up during the economic collapse of 2008 and the bailout that followed. As banks and foreign investors were being made whole, getting their principals back dollar for dollar, average Americans were asked to grovel at the doorstep of the very same financial institutions that had required taxpayer money to stay afloat.

Had there been any fairness at all in the system, then the credit card rates of Americans holding cards issued from TARP institutions should have been rolled back to rates equal to the usury laws. Back in the day, banks were made exempt from usury laws, because they were considered responsible financial institutions and not loan sharks. When it became clear that they were not responsible, this should have been the very first reaction, lifting the usury exemption for any financial institutions requiring TARP funds. Interestingly, no one in government offered it as an option.

Admittedly, usury law is an obscure sector of the credit world, but only because BankAmericard and MasterCharge changed the credit landscape so dramatically in the 1970s. When they issued generic plastic credit cards the systemic structures necessary to facilitate today's crisis were put in place. Besides lifting the usury exemption, we should have extended to every American in a troubled mortgage the option for support from the same taxpayers that propped up the institutions that were too big to fail. There is absolutely no reason why Americans cannot support other Americans except average Americans are no longer an interest group that politicians pay attention to. Instead of the lame mortgage modifications that are allegedly being offered to Americans, but seem to rarely actually happen, why not invest directly in individuals. To invest directly in Americans in trouble would seem to be the right thing to do.

This is how such an investment program would work. If an American refinanced during the window of greatest exploitation and corruption, say 2005 through 2008, and they are now on the verge of foreclosure, then the American taxpayer would invest in them by paying off the back mortgage payments. If the homeowner could not make the monthly payment, rather than reduce the principal, the taxpayers would subsidize the homeowner's mortgage up to a ceiling of perhaps 25%. Homeowners who take advantage of the program would be required to hold onto the house for 5-10 years after the bailout. The back mortgage payments and subsidies would be a stake invested by the taxpayers and when the asset sold the taxpayer's would get their fair share. Homeowners requiring a monthly stipend to make their monthly mortgage payment would be required to sell their house within ten years, if they were unable to wean themselves from the stipend within the ten-year window.

There is a certain amount of administrative overhead to the aforementioned mortgage bailout program, but the idea of fairness should matter. After all, most Americans were not responsible for the financial crisis that befell the nation. It was the bankers and other big money players that created the disaster. American taxpayers investing in American taxpayers makes incredible sense, but so far no one has floated the idea because the true constituents of today's politicians see absolutely no positive in such a plan.

We cannot ignore our debts as we make these investments though. We must deal with our debt, before our creditors force us to do so. If we have invested wisely, we have a chance of being on the upturn economically when the fiscal day of reckoning comes. We may even be able to ignore our creditors, because we will no longer owe them. A stronger economy, publicly and privately, will give us the strength we need to ward off economic doom.

To invest in our infrastructure and ourselves over the longer term we must begin to pay down our debt as well. Given the size of our military obligations around the world, it will take years to draw down these expeditionary forces deployed across the world, but withdraw we must. Our budgetary woes leave this nation no choice, but to draw down these foreign occupations as fast as possible. Until we do, we continue to hemorrhage money at an incredible rate while doing nothing to build our own economy. Military interventions do nothing for infrastructure. Additionally, post war veteran benefits are a poorly accounted future entitlement that will not be small and needs to be honored. We will be paying these military entitlements for decades to come. Unfortunately, we really have not done the calculations as to the true cost of these entitlements.

To start paying down our debt, we should institute a VAT. A value added tax of a penny or two will be a load on our economy, but at least it will be applied evenly on all citizens. Given our multi-trillion dollar economy, a two-cent VAT could yield a trillion dollars to be applied against our debt in a few years. The VAT should be mandated by law to pay down the national debt. A large portion of that debt is held in the Social Security Trust Fund and it should be at the top of the list of items to be paid off.

Once we have paid our debts down to zero, we can then discuss whether a VAT would be preferred over the current income tax. There are many things to consider, such as whether the elimination of the mortgage interest deduction would further destroy the housing market. There will be many competing interests in this debate, but it will be a problem of success...a successful paying down of America's debt will be the catalyst.

Immigration

The immigration question in the U.S. can really be distilled down
to the Mexicans and then everyone else. That is a reality that we
must deal with as a practical matter when considering the
immigration issue in the United States. South and Central America
of course contribute mightily, but the rest of the world does so
also. Mexico is our neighbor on top of being the heaviest
contributor of immigrants. They are the majority of the
immigrants, and we must solve this "problem" with Mexico first. It
is not as intractable an issue in the same way that global warming,
erosion of civil liberties, joblessness, and the militarization of our
economy are, because most everyone agrees on the essential nature
of the problem, undocumented immigration into the US. Still there
is complexity related to the many businesses profiting from illegal
labor and a general feeling of invasion from American citizens.
This invasion feeling needs to be addressed by progressives.

Amnesty for Mexicans brought to this country illegally by
their parents is the morally correct course. Once upon a time,
America cared about such ethical issues and strove to take the
humane course whenever possible. Americans should also consider
that this undocumented generation could help rescue America from
the demographic time bomb that our aging populace represents.
This in fact is America's secret weapon against many of her
competitors in the world, especially the Chinese. China's one child
policy has increased the average age of their population
significantly. Amnesty for this innocent and youthful segment of
the undocumented is practical, compassionate and energizes
America. Amnesty for their parents makes sense as well for many
of the same reasons.

Americans could be helped to find their compassionate sides
by considering a brief history of Mexican-American relations
during the last 150 years. Such a consideration yields some

surprising facts concerning American interventions into Mexico by our military. Mexico is the Third World right on our doorstep and perhaps America should acknowledge her role in her neighbor's plight. The economic dichotomy is especially stark along our borders. A short trip on the highway is all that separates a future of hopeless poverty in Mexico and one of limitless opportunity in the USA.

At best, America has ignored and, at worst, has been at war with our southern neighbor. America must defuse the growing social unrest in Mexico. The people of Mexico have known little freedom and even less prosperity over the past two centuries. America bears some responsibility for the current state of affairs. In the 1840s, we picked a fight with the inferior army of Mexico. Both candidates, in the American election of 1840, supported war with the newly independent Mexico. The more strident of the two, Polk, won. America claimed a Manifest Destiny. We were destined to stretch from sea to shining sea, and we did not care whom we ran over in the process.

The excuse for the war was the annexation of Texas, which had seceded from Mexico five years earlier, but had always wished to be a part of the United States rather than independent. This made sense, because the leaders of the Texas revolution were transplanted Americans. Texas was the pretense, but Polk definitely wanted more. California, Arizona, and New Mexico were all on his list for acquisition.

We invaded from the north, and simultaneously in the south, we landed Marines in Vera Cruz. From Vera Cruz, despite heavy Mexican resistance led by Santa Anna, we took Mexico City. We forced Mexico to sell the American Southwest at a price we deemed fair. It is the height of foolishness to believe that the Mexican people do not still remember this war with great bitterness. Mexicans do not see immigration as an act of invasion, but rather one of reclamation.

In 1916, Germany sought to tap these feelings of resentment in Mexicans and ignite anger against America, but it backfired. The secret telegram sent by a high official in Germany, named Zimmermann, to Mexico fell into the hands of an American newspaper. The notorious "Zimmermann Note" was published, and the American public was enraged. In the telegram, Germany offers the return of California, Arizona, and Texas if the Mexicans will enter into an alliance against the United States.

Germany had good reason to believe that Mexico would be interested. After all, there was an American army running around Northern Mexico in 1916. General, "Black Jack" John J. Pershing, who later led the American Expeditionary Force into WWI, commanded the army in Mexico. With a foreign force occupying their land, Germany was not wrong to believe they could energize Mexican opposition to the US.

Pershing was chasing the rebel, Pancho Villa. Villa had crossed the border and attacked Columbus, New Mexico, killing Americans. Villa's motivations are complex. There had been a popular revolution in Mexico near the turn of the century. Emilio Zapata and Villa were rebel generals in this revolution. After much fighting, a rather weak president was installed in Mexico City. The situation was stable for a while, but when the president was assassinated amid rumors of American involvement, the country was thrown into turmoil once again. Zapata and Villa, among others, took up arms again. Villa controlled much of Northern Mexico.

Unfortunately, the seat of government was in Mexico City, which was in the South. America chose to support those that had gained control in Mexico City. President Wilson allowed troops from Mexico City to use American railroads to attack Villa's rear flank. This infuriated Villa. He declared war on the United States and attacked the small border town of Columbus.

President Woodrow Wilson ordered Pershing to bring Villa in for trial. For months, Pershing chased Villa. There were a number of skirmishes, but nothing conclusive. As Germany became ever more belligerent and Mexico ever more fragmented, Wilson brought his general home so that he could go to Europe for WWI. The Mexicans fought on among themselves, and eventually, a government was formed.

Though the constitution of Mexico is based on ours, the Mexican people have not known much freedom. Dictators, crooks, and incompetents in high places have plagued them. Mexico has been her own worst enemy down through the years, but still some responsibility falls on the shoulders of America to help her to feed and house her people. We annexed some of the richest lands in the entire world. California is the eighth largest economy in the world, and Texas is not far behind.

The disaster of the Mexican economy is appalling. Tourists that venture outside the confines of their resort in Mexico are shocked by the poverty of the common people. Many live quite literally in tarpaper and sheet metal shacks with no running water. The economy offers the people, especially in the northern part of the nation, little in the way of opportunities to improve their lot. No wonder they are willing to brave any obstacle for a better life in the United States. After seeing the conditions in Tijuana firsthand, many no longer condemn these people to their hopeless lives. They suddenly understand the desperation of Mexico's poor. Some even come to the incredible conclusion that these people should be allowed to come across the border freely. Progressives as students of American history will realize that allowing Mexicans into the U.S. is almost an obligation given our past tampering with the politics of our southern neighbor.

This free access should only apply to Mexican citizens. America must face her past sins and make adequate penance so that she can move on. The Mexican War was an ugly chapter in American history. Suitably documented and tracked, Mexicans should be allowed to live and work in America, as long as they wish, with some limitations. We should also fast track Mexicans who wish to become American citizens, because they can be a positive demographic force in our society. America's future requires us to face our past and make amends.

The opening of the border could be a gradual thing, phased over a number of years. Americans should realize that the USA actually needs an influx of young, new immigrant blood. Our tax base is shrinking. Demographically, America is turning gray. Immigrants could inject significant tax dollars into our federal budget for many years to come. To really fix Social Security and Medicare over the long term an influx of young and fertile Mexicans is almost a requirement.

Our southern border has been called the Cactus Curtain and progressives will tear it down. Any Mexican that takes the time to learn English should be allowed in and put on a path to citizenship. A simple high school English exam will suffice as an immigration screen. We could extensively document each Mexican who wishes to come into the United States. With such an open border with our neighbor, we need not worry about ordinary Mexicans sneaking in. Additionally, we will have documented them so thoroughly as to make it easy to permanently deport them, if necessary.

The Border States are bearing a heavy burden. Illegal aliens are taxing state services, yet they cannot receive federal money for the undocumented persons. By managing the influx closely, we can also keep them off the welfare rolls. Many only wish to work for a while and then go home to their families with a nest egg. Such an open border seems a small reparation to pay for compelling Mexico to sell California, Arizona, New Mexico, and Texas against their will. Likely many Mexicans will wish to stay and eventually gain full citizenship and this will complete the healing process that needs to happen between our two countries.

Progressives realize that we need to institute this policy if we do not want to have to invade Mexico again to put down popular revolt. That is what the intense poverty and drug violence down there is currently breeding. The people of Mexico remember the past, and they desperately want a future. Such a policy need not lead to greater unemployment. The economy is already absorbing an immense number of illegals, each of whom are working two and three jobs so that argument is specious.

Our nation was built on immigration. Many of our greatest technological leaps in science have come from immigrant minds. Albert Einstein and Werner von Braun leap to the forefront at the shallowest consideration of this point. To those who say that our economy cannot handle such unbridled immigration, they should consider the following: we do not know what diamonds in the rough we are condemning to a mind-numbing existence in the ghettos of Mexico. The next Einstein may be wearing diapers in Tecate, Mexico.

To reap the benefits of Mexican's boundless energy and help them make better lives for themselves in the process, America should embrace Mexican workers that can pass an English test and want to become American citizens. Otherwise, we will pay with American blood for ignoring our southern neighbors and failing to give them a chance to be Americans. Progressives also realize that embracing our southern neighbor will require tolerance.

In addition, there are some other aspects to the immigration debate that are worth considering, such as H1B visas. These visas allow big corporations to practice labor arbitrage under the guise of bringing in the best and the brightest from overseas. There is much talk of the proper skillsets not being available in the American worker pool, so these visas are necessary. However, this is very shortsighted, because it will require us to continually issue more and more H1B visas. The domestic workforce will continue to lag behind, since no serious effort is made to train the American work force.

These damages to our workforce are not predictions anymore. Essentially that is what has happened over the last 20 years. This type of immigration is very destructive, because these visa holders tend to be nothing more than indentured servants who do as their employer says to avoid being deported. Indentured servants are much different from real immigrants like Einstein who became American citizens and knew the rights of that citizenship.

Corporate America wants these H1B changes to be part of any broad immigration reform related to illegal alien labor coming from the south, for obvious reasons. After all, it is very tough to balance work and family with deadlines and overtime. Sometimes those darn uppity American workers want to be with their families. The more unpaid overtime that can be squeezed out of a worker, the greater the profits and productivity numbers driving executive bonuses. We can imagine the realities that those H1B workers face. If the boss says to work 50 or 60 hours for 75% of the normal salary, you do it or you could be back in the homeland, right quick.

Another point to consider is the fact that Americans can sometimes be unwilling to spy on their fellow citizens. Americans born into the Land of the Free know that a government spying on its own citizens is not free. An American blew the whistle on the Bush administration's data mining operations. An H1B visa holder would never jeopardize their visa by publically revealing such unconstitutional behavior. One must wonder whether federal support for H1B visas might also allow for a more compliant workforce to build out domestic surveillance networks.

Now the arguments about the lack of skills in the American workforce may have some weight, but the "Just in Time" hiring practiced by American corporations has been tough on American workers. In-demand employees have learned to stay with an employer willing to give them a fair shake at a fulltime W-2 job rather than jump to the next big salary. This desire for job stability makes American workers less likely to be useful fodder for the "Just in Time" employment machine, hence another reason corporate America wants more H1B visas.

Additionally, it has been almost twenty years since the alleged high tech skillset shortage was identified. Had we invested in our own citizens then, we would have been much better off today, but Corporate America pursues short-term profits rather than long-term American economic health. With Corporate America driving policy, we are facing pervasive structural unemployment. This unemployment will only get worse unless we make long-term investments in our own people, instead of always taking the expedient course that corporations want to pursue.

The politicians have no vision here, but simply serve their corporate masters desire to practice labor arbitrage. This labor arbitrage continues to drive down the wages of the American worker.

In the final analysis, this cannot end well for the nation. It takes a clear, patriotic vision to take the short-term heat of making sure the American workforce is protected and trained. There will be a strong push to sneak in labor arbitrage friendly regulations into any solution to our porous southern border. Progressives will provide a clear vision and focus to bring practical solutions to the Mexican-American relationship while still protecting the American worker from corporate exploitation.

The Case Against Torture

Nothing has cost us our standing internationally like the violations of the Geneva Convention that America has perpetrated over the last ten years. We have completely lost the moral high ground. Not only do progressives believe torture is morally wrong, progressives think it is actually ineffective, especially over the long haul.

The case for torture has been supported through many hyperbolic hypothetical scenarios, where torture seems to be the only correct answer. For example, consider this hypothetical situation: one knows where an individual has kidnapped one's family and is holding them hostage. Given such knowledge, one would not want to give such an individual a big wet liberal kiss, pat them on the head, and coo about their troubled childhoods. No, one's actions are not likely to be so socially considerate. Would one not torture them? Well, yes, of course one would, in the most horrible of ways if they chose not to cooperate by revealing the information as to the captive family members.

The Geneva Convention would not bind such a person. Additionally, in this case, one would have some kind of real proof in their own mind that the individual had the piece of knowledge one needed to free one's beloved family. Without that, an ordinary person could not summon the necessary ruthlessness. Additionally, if they were wrong, the consequences would be severe and the torturer would bear that price whether their actions were discovered or not.

That is why torture cannot be institutionalized, because torture is a very personal thing, a personal decision, at the moment, in the heat of battle. Without this personal touch, there is born a bureaucracy of torture, disconnecting the personal nature of what is being done. Make no mistake, the torturer is irreparably damaged by their actions just as the victim suffers damage. When that decision is made to cross the line and torture, the psychological impact on the torturer is no small consequence. It should not be something that is ordered by a commander in the "civilized" military of a "civilized" nation. That is why the military establishment of this country wants us to adhere to the Geneva Convention. Let us not forget that our soldiers are ordinary people and would like to stay that way.

In the progressive worldview, the granularity of the command structure of the military, echoes the social paradigm and goes down to the individual level. Ultimately, the individual can only handle some decisions in the here and now. If, for example, one can immediately extract information from someone by an "enhanced" interrogation that immediately saves many lives, well, perhaps military brass looks the other way. Maybe they won't give the interrogator a medal, but they would understand the sacrifice that had been made by the citizen soldier for his country and his buddies. On the other hand, if the brass hears of mistreatment, it must always investigate and punish "enhanced" interrogation tactics. Higher-ups must especially investigate when these actions bear no immediate fruit, or are otherwise unjustified, to prevent the temptations of the darkest of human places during the hell of war.

It is only in this immediate fog of war, where individuals have to make snap value decisions that "enhanced" interrogation might yield some immediate salvation for their comrades or civilians. The military institution must always explicitly frown and discourage torture to prevent the moral and ethical destruction of their own soldiers. This is one of the strongest reasons for always adhering to the Geneva Convention officially, while understanding that in the hell of war many things happen.

Official and institutionalized torture destroys the very real and practical benefits that can occasionally come from the horrific practice of torturing a prisoner. To be honest, torture may have its place during life and death decisions that occur on the battlefield in very special circumstances, but without this type of immediacy, the torture becomes ineffective anyway. Enemy comrades would know that when an individual is captured, they would be tortured. They know what their comrade knows, and they begin to rearrange their strategies, their structures of communication, their locations for hiding, etc.

Guerilla military units are set-up to be able to fly apart and come back together as if magnetized. When torture is the normal modus operandi of one's opponents, then military leaders make sure to keep individuals only lightly informed, so that there is little they can reveal. In fact, wily guerillas are steeped in misinformation to spout during torture. The results of such misinformation would lead to their torturers wasting time chasing the ghosts of the torture interrogation.

The enemies of America now expect to be tortured. Oh, how horrible it is to write, but Americans cannot deny it! Our enemies now expect to be tortured and it is hard to argue that they are wrong to expect it. Even when we deny that we torture, enough evidence has come to light along with confirming admissions from our officials that our enemies expect to be tortured and train accordingly.

How do we explain to our kids that we are the good guys when our enemies are trained to hold out against American torture interrogation tactics? Since our enemies are likely training their people to expect this treatment, our tactics can rarely if ever uncover anything normal interrogation techniques would not have uncovered. Probably they have two or three layers of lies that they go through to get the torture to stop for that day. After all, our people then have to go out and investigate the veracity of the information. Each day that the tortured stops the torture is a victory for him. Each day that the prisoner buys for his comrades is a victory to a person that is willing to die for the cause, the homeland, the fatherland or whatever it is.

Institutionalized torture simply does not work! There is no real evidence after a decade of use that it works over the long haul. Institutionalized torture by a government or military bureaucracy is ineffective. The aforementioned are the rational, empirical, and logical reasons behind a particular society or nation's support of the Geneva Convention.

However, torture is not about rational and logical behavior. Passions on this issue run high and to many torture is the vilest of evils, but not all. The passions surrounding torture can be used for political gain. The torturers can use torture as a propaganda tool to elicit positive emotions about the strength and power of the ruling party and the military. The torturers claim to be making the tough decisions necessary to protect America, but this is not clear. There seemed a political smell to the timing of the Bush/Cheney rejection of the Geneva Convention that was meant to appeal to their cowboy narrative. A narrative that was little more than a morality tale of the good guys versus the bad guys that led to pre-emptive invasions against two countries.

For progressives there is no real moral dilemma here at all. If the enemy is willing to die, then he is willing to be tortured, and we have now willingly taken the battle to the darkest of places. By torturing, you lose the high ground in the battle of ideas, in the battle for souls. In the final analysis, torture does not work, but it is also immoral and the latter reason used to prevent us from even debating the former.

During Britain's darkest hour, as the forces of the Third Reich lapped at her shores, George Orwell eloquently discounted any talk of stooping to the level of the Nazis. Few would dispute that the free world was on the brink during World War II, there was certainly no less at stake then than there is now. Nonetheless, when the despicable actions of the Nazis against British POWs agitated the British as to forget their moral and ethical underpinnings, the following Orwellian essay allowed cooler heads to prevail.

> *"May I be allowed to offer one or two reflections on the British Governments' decision to retaliate against German prisoners, which seems so far to have aroused extraordinarily little protest? By chaining up German prisoners in response to similar action by the Germans, we descend, at any rate in the eyes of the ordinary observer, to the level of our enemies. It is unquestionable when one thinks of the history of the past ten years that there is a deep moral difference between democracy and Fascism, but if we go on the principle of an eye for an eye and a tooth for a tooth, we simply cause that difference to be forgotten. Moreover, in the matter of ruthlessness, we are unlikely to compete successfully with our enemies. As the Italian radio has just proclaimed, the Fascist principle is two eyes for an eye and a whole set of teeth for one*

tooth. At some point or another, public opinion in England will flinch from the implications of this statement, and it is not very difficult to foresee what will happen. As a result of our action, the Germans will chain up more British prisoners, we shall have to follow suit by chaining up more Axis prisoners, and so it will continue till logically all the prisoners on either side will be in chains. In practice, of course, we shall become disgusted with the process first, and we shall announce that the chaining up will now cease, leaving, almost certainly, more British than Axis prisoners in fetters. We shall have thus acted both barbarously and weakly, damaging our own good name without succeeding in terrorising the enemy. It seems to me that the civilised answer to the German action would be something like this: 'You proclaim that you are putting thousands of British prisoners in chains because some half-dozen Germans, or thereabouts, were temporarily tied up during the Dieppe raid. This is disgusting hypocrisy, in the first place because of your own record during the past ten years, in the second place because troops who have taken prisoners have got to secure them somehow until they can get them to a place of safety, and to tie men's hands in such circumstances is totally different from chaining up a helpless prisoner who is already in an internment camp. At this moment, we cannot stop you maltreating our prisoners, though we shall probably remember it at the peace settlement, but don't fear that we shall retaliate in kind. You are Nazis, we are civilised men. This latest act of yours simply demonstrates the difference.' At this moment this may not seem a very satisfying reply, but I suggest that to anyone who looks back in three months' time, it will seem better than what we are doing at present, and it is the duty of those who can keep their heads to protest before the inherently silly process of retaliation against the helpless is carried any further."

~ George Orwell 1942

Orwell's eloquent rejection of torture would be criticized as quaint naiveté in the 21st century. The experiences of World War II, and its immediate aftermath, color the American vision of war and this is understandable, but it is no longer related to us first hand. It truly was one of the greatest triumphs of America, and it was a shared victory through all levels of society. Certainly, no political party or philosophy was overly represented among the military victors as all stripes of Americans had been drafted or enlisted. The egalitarian reality of that war and the real military experiences are being lost as most of the soldiers from World War II have now passed on. That loss of the personal experiences of those veterans of the greatest generation prevents Americans from tapping that shared sacrifice experience that used to unite us. An entire generation of men knew the ugly face of war, sought to avoid it if possible and were members of each political party in equal numbers. Torture was never anything these veterans ever believed would be sanctioned by their own government.

Without the wisdom of this generation, Americans now hear an unverified mythology about the Second World War. We suffer as a nation without the personal testimony from trusted relatives that bring insight from WWII. Insights that help us understand how the Geneva Convention is more than a quaint notion and is actually something that is essential for a civilized nation to respect.

Campaign Reform

Our process of electing our national leaders is awash in money. The process is corrupted by big money. We all know this, and campaign reform is regularly on the national agenda. However, no matter what laws are passed, real reform escapes us. One of the positives about a bigger House of Representatives, as advocated in this book, is that it will take much more money to control voting majorities in a House with many hundreds of new members. Increasing the size of the House will bring about a kind of campaign reform. Taking the money out of politics is nearly impossible, but we will mitigate the effects by making those that would buy their legislation have to pay for more votes.

The political duopoly of Republican/Democrat is very much a part of the problem, as well. The Founding Fathers never envisioned the amount of influence political parties wield over the American election process. The political parties will continue into the future and wield their power in the selection of candidates. Political partisanship has served its purpose over the years by creating a push/pull in the debate that brings about compromise and builds consensus. Unfortunately, of late, the bipolar and strident nature of the debate leaves no room for nuance and change, and it has caused forward motion to slowly stop. Political partisanship loves the status quo and political gridlock is guaranteeing that the status quo will continue.

One reason that American politics has become so divisive is the growing efficiency of software to gerrymander a political district, especially at the House of Representative level. Political parties use their vast resources to redraw the Congressional districts every ten years. With ever more computing power and data granularity, politicians can draw districts that create just the right demographic to get them re-elected. This has helped widen the great bipartisan divide by virtually eliminating moderate, blended, centrist districts.

Progressives should push legislation to rein in the software driven gerrymandering dividing our electorate. Through an objective analysis of population distribution within the United States, we can limit Congressional districts and the software that defines them to first honor current political divisions at the local level before radical redrawing would be allowed. This means that a district would not likely cut through five or more cities, but rather adhere more closely to the existing city boundaries. In unincorporated areas, county boundaries would be the grassroots lines that the software would need to attempt to encompass within districts.

Limiting gerrymandering to something that more closely adheres to the local political boundaries at the grassroots levels of politics will have a profound effect. Politicians may be forced to advocate positions that are more moderate when their district is more diverse. This will surely be helpful in ending gridlock. However, nothing can substitute for an engaged electorate, and some updated selection processes should help bring about this engagement.

When the majority of the electorate chooses to no longer identify with either Democrat or Republican, there is obviously a growing discontent with the duopoly. Perhaps, a new Progressive political party will make sense to fill this void, but embracing the independent voter citizen as a sort of party makes sense too. The ground is as fertile as it ever has been for a progressive agenda to grab the support of a new Silent Majority. A united, solid majority could bring about an American Renaissance in both the private and public sectors, without necessarily founding a new political party.

Progressives must put their faith in the citizen-voter, and that means getting more people into the election process without requiring huge amounts of money and the party apparatus that collects it. As a nation, we need a selection process that is more egalitarian for federal offices. Our current process is too exclusive, and we can use technology and 21st-century American culture to broaden it.

We need a more engaged electorate to transform American politics. How to achieve this is hardly a clear course. There is a need for some speculative vision here. The larger House definitely brings more opportunities for individuals to break onto the national stage, but we can guarantee an influx of fresh faces into government through a publicly funded campaign process for independent citizen-voters.

America is in its third century, and technology is actively changing the world. There is a real need for a flexible vision on how America can regain her greatness. Earlier in this chapter and in those that came before there have been very specific policy recommendations, but from here things become a bit more nebulous and visionary.

Technology could be leveraged to engage the electorate. To bring more citizens into the system, we would bring random selections of citizens to compete against their current Congressman every two years. The process will be similar to jury pool selection, and it will require true randomness to work.

To make it manageable, we would count all congressional districts from 1 to 435, or how ever many are currently extant at the time of the first cycle and then randomly select districts for "regular" people candidacies. Congressional elections are held every two years, so we could extend the process over a decade by selecting districts ending in 0 or 1 in the first cycle, ending in 2 and 3 in the second cycle, and until 8 and 9 in the fifth cycle, ten years in. At the end of ten years, congressional districts would be renumbered again, and the whole ten-year cycle would begin anew. This pattern distributes the "citizen-compete" districts all across the nation. This scheme also limits the number of new citizen politicians to a maximum of just 20% that could be elected, if they won every race.

In each district, a pool of individuals would be selected randomly from the congressional district, similar to jury pool selections. These individuals would then be treated like "American Idol" contestants, but in a political arena. As dangerous as it sounds, it is a powerful way to engage the electorate as participants as well as constituents. Progressives must increase the Power of the People, and success is measured by the extent that the people actually participate. Engagement of the electorate is a primary goal. If the people do not pay attention and exercise their power, it evaporates or is subverted, and the late 20th century has been quite illustrative of this point.

Initially, the process will be publicly funded out of the general fund to seed the candidates. FCC licenses will contain provisions to compel broadcasters to provide free airtime on some kind of rating schedule to spread the burden. Broadcasters will provide airtime not just for traditional political advertising, but also for a publicly funded selection process that will be televised for each congressional district involved. The primaries of the publicly funded congressional selection process within a given district would follow the reality TV voting model.

Panels of journalists, politicians, and others deemed appropriate by locals will form small panels to ask questions of the candidates. These panels will help drive the process, but the call-in voting format of reality television would be driving the selection. Voters will be charged a nominal fee per vote, perhaps a nickel, to provide a campaign fund after final votes are tabulated. A nickel to get your voice heard will appeal to Americans, and the money will fund a war chest for the ultimate winner/candidate of this people-powered process. Additionally, technology can be used to prevent the gaming of elections by making sure that the calling phone number is registered to a voter within the congressional district that is being contested. In fact, creating a transparent and verifiable electronic voting model is necessary anyway due to the amount of irregularities that we have seen in the electronic voting machines since their introduction.

We are constantly reminded of the need for new ideas in a new century, and though progressives believe fervently in the wisdom of the Founding Fathers, they also recognize the need for the nation to adapt to a new and changing world. Therein lies the true wisdom of our founders, because the Constitution can be amended; there is flexibility if necessary. Though, in this case, there is likely no need for constitutional amending. Political parties were able to gain their power through the wide-open nature of elections as defined in the Constitution. Admittedly, political parties will not be supportive of this process, but as all branches of the governmental apparatus evolve and our society evolves, our candidate selection process should evolve and reflect the original egalitarian ideas of the founders. That is the basis for proposing this American Idol-style election cycle.

Given the incredibly drastic changes that our society has undergone, we all see the need for some evolution. That evolution extends to the electorate itself as well. A publicly funded primary process for citizen-candidates will only work if the electorate chooses to participate in the election process. If people can vote on "American Idol" and "Dancing with the Stars", then surely they can find the time to listen to public primary candidates for their congressional representative once every ten years.

The future of American Greatness is dependent upon her citizenry embracing their civic duties; otherwise, Power to the People falls flat. Surely, it is speculative that such a process will inject local candidates into the House of Representatives and engage people. Hope springs eternal and thankfully, a candidate that is elected through this process need not owe any allegiance to a partisan hierarchy. The parties will fight this reform and argue that they are the experts at candidate selection. Scare tactics will rule the day as the parties attempt to hold their duopoly, but progressives will put their faith in the people as the agents of change that break that duopoly.

This competing publicly funded campaign candidate selection process will also facilitate transparency in electronic voting. Voting machines across the nation are insecure and allow for no paper receipt that allows the voter to check that their ballot is being counted properly. Electronics allow for the gaming of elections in ways the paper process can never support. In a paper election, fraud generally requires a candidate to at least be close to winning. With electronic fraud in elections, there is no such practical limitation. The publicly funded independent candidate selection process will require such voter audits to move forward.

The opposition that the duopolists will bring to a publicly funded independent candidate selection process will bear some positive fruit when it comes to transparency. Without a truly transparent selection process that allows for close auditing of votes an American Idol-like selection process will not be able to pass muster. That will mean that voter auditable and 3rd party audit trails of vote tabulation will be an absolute requirement. A great dividend of this process will be these electronic checks and balances will have to be pushed into the current electoral process. That dividend will be addressing the much less transparent voting machines with their non-existent audit trails that have plagued our nation in the 21st century.

The Vision Thing

The Progressive Vision

The vision thing is often in short supply when it is most needed. We currently lack national vision about where we are going and what we believe as a nation. There are many interest groups that would claim to hold the rights to the message of what is believed by this nation, but the fact is none of those interest groups can speak for a solid majority any more. Each has their narrow vision of what a proper, patriotic and capitalist American ought to believe. This vision may allow them to have a stable core of passionate believers, but no governing majority. Today's competing visions are so narrow that they cannot claim a large solid majority that can govern in the way that our democratic representative republic was designed to operate.

After empowering the people and instituting specific policy, progressives still need a foundational vision that acts as a moral and ethical compass going forward. A progressive vision of individual freedom and tolerance provides a flexible framework for considering future social evolution. Freedom and tolerance are necessary to prevent us from tearing ourselves apart as time goes by. Progressives worry about America, but believe in her inherent durability. Progressives refuse to accept the contention that we should abandon the basic ideals of individual freedom and liberty despite the signs of an epic collapse.

There are clear signs that America is on the wrong path, but we can change course. The Roman Republic lasted 500 years before it descended into empire and dictatorship. America, our great experiment, is only a couple of hundred years old; there is still historical precedent for the U.S. to continue to thrive. Progressives believe the ideals of America are stronger than any society in history, because we are more diverse, more energetic and more tolerant than those that came before. America can still lead the world to the promised land of peace and prosperity, but her citizens must rise to the challenge of that leadership.

At the end of the 20th century, America was poised to lead the world to that hoped for place of peace and global teamwork. We were the lone superpower, and the Iron Curtain had fallen. In the Balkans, we had prevented the Serbians from reigniting European nationalism and genocide. America headed up a NATO military force, which acted to stop the conflict in the former Yugoslavia. Peace reined, and an era of Pax Americana appeared to be real. The ideals of republican capitalism and freedom were no longer in doubt at the end of the 20th century. The future seemed wide open to incredible possibilities, as we realized that the destructive setbacks of large, regional and global military conflicts could be a thing of the past.

In this brave new world of the late 1990s, there was such a dearth of bad news, we got off course. With so much peace around the world, our partisan political system lacked the usual crazy antics that used to fuel ratings for news shows. They needed to fill the airwaves with vitriol and hyperbole to get attention and ratings, but things were going relatively well in America and the world. Perhaps Americans were bored or just lacked the vision to maximize the opportunity, but for some reason we did not use our economic, moral and military high ground to bring the world together in a more peaceful coexistence. Instead, we went on a lunatic destruction of our own leadership through the Lewinsky investigations, spearheaded by Ken Starr. Our self-destruction came at a time when we could have been investing our country's budget surplus in vital infrastructure or social goals, but we spent our time chasing sex scandals. The tawdry political tales got American attention, and so they made money for advertisers and gave politicians something to rail against, but they did nothing to further our national agenda.

Coming into the 21st century, Americans actually seemed to miss the sexploitation dramas that surrounded Clinton once he left office. Without a vision of America's true role as a beacon of freedom and individual liberty, we went looking for salacious stories at all levels of our political arena in 2001. Lest we forget, the entertainment themed news shows were filled with a lurid narrative about the Democratic Congressman Gary Condit and his murdered intern, Chandra Levy, in the summer of 2001. Right up until the planes crashed into the buildings on September 11th of that fateful year, the Condit/Levy affair was the lead story. In the summer of 2001, we had no earth-shattering problems when compared to the seemingly insurmountable mess that we now face. Today, at the edge of an economic abyss, in a world full of turmoil and war, we have no time for R-rated stories of adultery, sex, and kneepads.

Make no mistake the vision thing has a very strong personal aspect to it. Most political vision starts with one person or a small group of people. In this the more speculative visionary portion of the book, the progressive vision does have a strong personal flavor to it. In this section, the formal 3rd person narrative will occasionally fall away, so that I may reveal the personal nature of this hopeful political vision. Politics is about people, so some personal aspects color the views of all. I think it is important for the readers to have some insights into the personal motivations of a political author with no real designs on public office. Why write all this if not to get elected?

The visions of America you read in this book are from a man who considered changing his citizenship from the United States. I was disgusted by the endless news cycles of sex and drug scandals; the cannibalization of our leadership seemed stupid and self-destructive. All the while, individual rights were being consistently eroded under the thin guise of public safety. During this time of personal political despair, I considered becoming a Canadian citizen. I explored the details of making such a citizenship change and reasoned it was feasible and doable to shed my American citizenship. However, in the end, I could not do it. I could not have my, as yet unborn, children not be Americans. I could not let go of being an American myself. America is an ideal that I could not abandon for my children or myself. (*Incidentally, I understand that, technically, we are United States citizens, but the world calls us Americans. We have always seen ourselves as Americans, and that is why I use the term throughout this book to refer to United States citizens.*)

Upon deep reflection, I still saw all the negative elements that made me want to flee and no longer be an American, but something inside prevented me from leaving this country. When I found that American deep inside, I realized I believed in the ideals too much. Things that I questioned about the Constitution and the

Bill of Rights when I first learned about them in school, because they seemed a danger to public safety, I now understood. As a student, when I first started hearing about and considering the Bill of Rights, much of it seemed a bit impractical and even naïve. By wrestling with the choice of citizenship, I found the Bill of Rights and embraced it passionately. The ideals of individual liberty and freedom, enshrined in that document, introduced the concept of a free citizen to a world of divine monarchies. I looked in the mirror, and I was an American. I believed in what the Founding Fathers preached, and I could not abandon it. My kids would be Americans with the red, the white, and the blue coursing through their veins, just like me. And this book and this vision were created as a gift to my children; all American children for that matter.

When I was born, America was in her hey-day, racing to put a man on the moon. Now, more than a decade after the birth of my first child, America is not in her hey-day. We are saddled by enormous debt. We are mired in military occupations of far-off lands. America is circling the drain. I cannot just turn my back. My children will be inheriting debt and disaster unless America can change course.

I keep telling myself that though there seems no hope, somehow, the people of America will pull it together. We will see our folly, and we will unite to return America to greatness. For the sake of my children's future, I have determined that I must believe in myself and trust my instincts. This agenda is the future of my children. Fueled by a parent's desire to make the world a better place for his children and a powerful patriotism that none can deny me, I have invested many hours and dollars to this enterprise. I truly believe the pen is mightier than any sword.

This is the plan. The pen will define the ideas. The ideas, the IDEAS; they will be the foot soldiers in our return to greatness. The idea that these pages can lay out a plan that will help America recapture herself, not by force, but by persuasive argument that defines American greatness. Even those that we fight and fear agree, for the Islamic prophet Muhammad is quoted as saying, "The ink of the scholar is holier than the blood of the martyr."

One of the few positives of the growing money problems our nation is facing is that there is now a greater willingness to put away our Islamaphobia and think outside the box to consider some new ideas. The political and social vision outlined in the preceding chapters, establishes the need to return more decision-making and representation to the people. The preceding chapters also provided specific policy positions that the people can support as large unassailable majorities in the near future.

Of course, there remain issues untouched so far that should be on everyone's radar screens as needing attention. Very specific policy recommendations remain elusive for some important issues of today. Not to mention those, yet undefined issues, that will arise in the future. These issues are important and consensus will need to be found. While on every issue of the day, it is impossible to provide the specificity that has come before in this book, one can still provide a progressive vision and some speculative future applications of that vision.

The Lost Legacy of Star Trek

Star Trek, the original series that only ran for three seasons has had an undisputed influence on the growth and direction of technology in America and in the world. There have been books and TV episodes dedicated to track the etymology of gadget after gadget to a particular Roddenberry-inspired device. This technological legacy has been documented elsewhere in detail, but many of the social messages and legacies have been lost and forgotten. Gene Roddenberry is one of the visionary thinkers of our time and I am heavily influenced by his vision, as our society is as a whole.

My passion for the TV show, "Star Trek – Original" runs deep. Maybe it was because I was born in 1962, so I was just at the right age, I do not know. That being said, I cannot deny that my ideas on foreign policy are influenced by the imagined future evolution of nationalism on the planet Earth. After all, for me, the Federation was where 1960s America was leading the globe and then the universe. In the Federation of that far future century, war had largely been done away with, though there was always the occasional skirmish to be worked out. Peace reigned on Earth.

At the time the series was canceled, few would have guessed how broadly and deeply the series has now penetrated our society. It is one of the legacies of a time when we had a single vision being pumped into our living rooms by the television. Much of "Star Trek" tech has found its way into our technological world, and engineers citing the show's influence on their ideas of what was possible often celebrate this. However, there was more there in that television series that should have made it into the "idea commons" of the American zeitgeist. I see the broader and greater legacy of the series as largely unfulfilled and ignored in the post-9/11 era.

There was a Russian on the bridge of the *Enterprise* during the height of the Cold War. Would there be a Muslim there today, or are we just too full of negative emotions to include a follower of Islam today on the bridge? Socially, the series was just as far advanced as it was technically. Martin Luther King actually implored Nichele Nichols to stay on the show when she told him that she was planning to abandon the Uhuru role. Martin Luther King convinced her of the social import of her role. He recognized the powerful social statements being made by Star Trek. Much of that social legacy is what is unfulfilled today and yet that was mostly what was so great about the series. The whiz-bang stuff was fantastic, but by setting things far in the future, Roddenberry could tackle difficult social issues from an objective distance and he did so with a phaser-like focus.

Kirk's long speeches about humanity's longing to be free rather than safe ring hollow in today's world of strip searches at the airport and CIA rendition. The Dignity of the Common Man, the real desire to let guilty men go free, rather than imprison one innocent man, were real ideals, real beliefs. They were time-honored, time-tested beliefs that taught us that despite the flaws, freedom and individual liberty were the best way to go even in the 23rd century.

There was a distinct libertarian vein in the plot lines. Those libertarian ideals have been almost completely lost in the real world. Can you imagine what Dr. McCoy would have said were Spock to advise the captain to torture a captive to obtain information?! In episode after episode, these basic ideas about humanity and the dignity of the individual are there, loudly proclaimed.

The all-powerful Federation was always forced to respect the dignity, not only of the common man, but also of the common sentient life form, no matter what their technological advancement. Could the "Prime Directive" stand up to today's torturous logic? Or would it be considered "quaint" like the Geneva Convention? We need only cue a William Shatner soliloquy to hear this vision of freedom and individual dignity eloquently and passionately espoused.

The real legacy of Star Trek is in danger of being lost. The Dignity of the Common Man was the most central theme and how that dignity had withstood hundreds of years of technological advancement. Through it all the essential rightness of it as a guiding principle never dimmed—or so predicted Gene Roddenberry of our future.

True fans of this series, who believed in it so fervently, should consider the deeper social message of the series and how it relates to today to help change the course of our nation. Americans need help understanding why they should stand up to the surveillance society. The fear-mongers will say we have to let the government turn this technology onto us, "to keep us safe". Progressives should promote the dignity of the individual in the way Gene Roddenberry did when we were young, but now is not here to do today.

Truly, this vision of freedom is the great legacy of Star Trek that should stand the test of time. Eventually, all the technological predictions will be far surpassed, and the interplay of the characters is all that is left. What Roddenberry was saying about the world, about the universe, was that no matter how the landscape changes, post 9/11 or not, there are certain guiding principles of humanity that will help get us through and that will set us apart in the greater universe.

We Need an American Commons

The 20th century brought tremendously homogenizing forces to bear upon the American society. World Wars and the Great Depression certainly marked the lives of all Americans, and these shared experiences were great unifying forces for sure. In addition to these historical events, radio and television created a daily, shared experience that printed materials, such as newspapers, had already begun to create in a limited way during the 19th century. Radio and television also brought real time reporting of big events from all over the nation to be experienced by all. Additionally, the state of these technologies meant that live reporting of events was difficult to fake in believable ways; Ronald Reagan's phantom baseball games notwithstanding.

The advent of television brought the ultimate unifying vision of current events at a time when video could not be easily manipulated. Television was quite empowering to the people, because when you saw a live broadcast of events, you could be reasonably sure that what was on the TV screen was happening on the scene—at least to a certain extent. Obviously, the choices of cameramen and editors of what to show did color that vision, but technology was not in a state that it could create a virtual reality.

Journalism and journalists approached levels of objectivity that we may never see again, because the images truly did the talking and the reporters just reported. The news was still seen as a public service function required for the network to retain their FCC licensing. News was a necessary cost of doing the business of creating content to put eyeballs on the TV set that could be sold to advertisers. An FCC license once required a broadcaster to engage in socially aware reporting to justify the broadcaster's retention of it.

At about the time that these homogenizing forces reached their zenith and brought about a true empowerment of the people, our society faced huge challenges. The sixties roared out of control, and the national nightmare of the JFK and RFK assassinations seeded doubts among the populace about whether their government was serving them or the interests of the moneyed and powerful.

The civil rights movement grew through television's reporting on the reality of inequality for blacks in the South. There is no question that this common witnessing, shared by all Americans, of what was occurring in the country and in our society, helped to move forward the civil rights movements that followed. The powerful eyes of the camera humanized the victims to groups that might never have been interested enough in their plight otherwise.

Today, we are faced with an ever-fragmenting vision of the country. Through personalization and marketing niches that allow us to hear and see only what we like, we have lost our common vision. Because people are now able to filter their media down to narrow streams of only what they like and want to see and hear, they become unaware of the "truths" that other Americans are living. "Truth" has become a point of view in America and is no longer a shared and universal truth.

People able to listen only to points of view they agree with reinforce narrow visions of "truth" that prevent the society-wide empathy that we desperately need. A more truthful portrayal of what it is to be an American today should help breed among us the equilibrium, egalitarianism, and tolerance that can resurrect an American Commons. All people can be in touch with this commons. When the idea of a commons disappears, we lose a lot as a society, like a shared infrastructure that we might all enjoy and maintain. These common shared things tie us together, but we must embrace them.

Progressives will draw from both parties redefining the political commons. Americans are separating into social networks occupied only by those that agree. These echo chambers are destroying the common social fabric that is essential to bind a nation together. Progressive roots in both parties can define a political social group that believes in the dignity of the individual over the state. Tolerance is required in a pluralistic vision of society. Progressive tolerance of all points of view can define an

American Commons where government of the people, by the people, and for the people nurtures political discourse. Elevating the individual over the state requires all to be equal under the law. Protecting the individual requires empathy for each other that is weakened in today's fragmented society. An inability for Americans to picture themselves in another citizen's shoes encourages the continuing growth of segregated, walled communities and gated corporate campuses. FCC licensing should encourage and reward efforts by media outlets to help create more common shared consumption of their content to change this.

The Dignity of the Common Man

One of the casualties in the destruction of a common American zeitgeist, a shared vision, was the idea of the Common Man. The concept of the "Dignity of the Common Man" is an important one. It is illustrative to consider the course of the extinction of the phrase and hence the idea. The phrase was edited out of television and movies just before the on-demand media age with hundreds of channels of content began to fragment the common media experiences of Americans. As the phrase disappeared from common parlance, so did the concept.

The phrase, dignity of the common man, was lost as feminism confronted our society's male chauvinism and began a campaign of sanitizing chauvinistic terms from our language. This is not to say that feminism is not a valid point of view. Surely, women needed to be granted their place, their dignity, and their freedom in our culture. However, the sanitation of our language of all chauvinistic phraseology and idioms had some negative consequences. The idea of the Common Man was an important one in striking a balance between the authorities and the individual. In the early days of the language purge, the appellation was perceived to be chauvinistic, but its death helped erode the concept of individual liberty in society.

The Dignity of the Common Man goes hand in hand with the genesis of the rule of law and egalitarianism. The loss of this powerful idea has helped erode individual liberty in favor of societal or statist goals. The Dignity of the Individual should be a 21st century catch phrase for the progressive movement. Progressives should attempt to tap the depth of common law understanding on individual liberty with this catchphrase. The Dignity of the Individual could help the resurrection of the concepts long defined as the Dignity of the Common Man. The old idea of the Dignity of the Common Man with our new, broader understanding of linguistic chauvinism might be resurrected, too.

It is this ideal of individual liberty that keeps judges in their role in the check and balance act between government and the individual citizen. This ideal to protect individuals from the coercive powers of the state should be the most basic fiber in the fabric that makes up the honorable judge's robes. The traditional idea behind the Dignity of the Common Man meant that a man's home truly was his castle, his freedom, his everything, making him in a sense equal to the king or the President as was so eloquently spelled out in the Magna Carta and then the Bill of Rights. Feminism helped change the dynamic in the old boys' network that made a police officer (a man) hesitant to break down the door of a citizen (a man) without the proper paperwork from a judge. This is not the fault of feminism, but it is a symptom of how society still has some problems dealing with the evolution of gender roles in society.

Without the support of the old boys' network of mutual male respect in a society ruled by law, it became easier to accept breakdowns of individual liberty in a society still not fully adjusted to new gender norms. Nowadays, the dignity of the individual is subject to numerous and varied attacks. Make no mistake the loss of mutual male respect did help break down individual liberty. The Dignity of the Individual American Citizen is something that will help turn back this erosion and reaffirm our confidence in individual freedom. Finding this common dignity means progressive Americans must bridge the gender gap and find the mutual gender respect that keeps individuals from infringing on each other's rights.

Militarization of America

The military-industrial complex has been a boom sector in 21st America. Despite President Dwight Eisenhower's expressed warnings to always be suspicious of the military-industrial complex, we find ourselves spending an enormous amount of money on the military. It is a shocking state of affairs given the clear and unambiguous words that General Eisenhower used in his farewell address, words like, "…conscious or unconscious manipulations of policy." Eisenhower understood that given the potential windfall that wartime profiteering could bring to business, many business leaders cannot help but be overly prejudiced toward military action. Remember Eisenhower had ended active combat operations in Korea and refused to take military action against the Soviets in Eastern Europe as well as stifling military involvement in Vietnam. The last president who was also a general had felt the pressure himself so much during his term that he practically called the defense industry unpatriotic and advised the American people perpetually to mistrust the military-industrial complex as he exited office.

One of the strongest consequences of the militarization of America is the shouting down of any civilian criticism of the military. On the street today and in the halls of Congress unless a person has served in the military their foreign policy opinions are discounted as naive. It seems today that advocating military action is the only "patriotic" opinion for a civilian. We should not be ashamed of being civilians. Americans should remember that we are a nation of civilians and that civil society is supposed to lead and restrain the military. A fact that Eisenhower felt he should emphasize on his exit.

When the general who won World War II spoke, one would expect Americans to listen, but the militarization of America has been a never-ending process. Without a persistent vigilance and energy from the citizenry, the military-industrial complex has become ever more powerful legislatively. As people power wanes and corporate power waxes in our government, the fact that almost every large corporation in America is making money from military contracts means that the defense industry is driving the debate in Washington, DC today. We have spent a decade at war, spending hundreds of billions today and incurring future financial obligations of incalculable proportions with almost nothing to show for it.

These future obligations are rarely discussed as part of the debate of defense spending, but they are very real and essentially unfunded. The military has been offering greater and greater incentives for enlistees and those that reenlist. Not only are taxpayers footing the bill as a nation for the care and feeding of the soldiers, which turns out to be a million dollars a year for each soldier to be deployed in Afghanistan or Iraq, we will ALSO pay for the health costs and education of their children decades into the future. These financial liabilities are unfunded and uncalculated obligations that we have on our books in addition to the other social entitlement programs we pay for. It is not that we should not pay the benefits, it is more about how these financial obligations are ignored as we try to balance our budget.

We are wasting so much money on foreign occupations and war, while we argue about spending fractions of these war costs on domestic infrastructure and social programs. We were told the invasion and occupation of Iraq would cost less than 100 billion dollars and that the Iraqis would fund it themselves from frozen assets. We have easily evaporated more than a trillion dollars in the last decade on war. In the final analysis, war does create short-term economic activity, but it creates no lasting infrastructure or other capitalized investment that will payoff far in the future.

Infrastructure investment is very expensive and does not necessarily give the same amount of short-term economic benefit that the defense industry can supply. Nonetheless, there are enormous long-term benefits, economic and otherwise from infrastructure investment. The payoffs of infrastructure investment simply cannot be calculated with any exactitude due to the difficulties of predicting the events of future decades. Nonetheless, these infrastructure investments most often do produce enormous future boosts to the economy. Two perfect examples of the huge dividends infrastructure investment can pay are the Republican Eisenhower's superhighway program or the rural electrification under the Democrat, FDR, as both of these still pay dividends today.

The costs of these foreign wars and long-term occupations of foreign lands justified on the pretext of making America safe are bankrupting our nation. We have been on a wartime footing for almost the entire 21st century. We have very little to show for these wars other than diminished prestige and bank accounts. Given the enormous technological advantages that we enjoyed, it is truly embarrassing that we have not won these military engagements decisively and in a timely fashion. This lack of victory speaks to an incredible incompetence or a purposeful desire by some for the military actions to continue. We have now fought for twice the length of World War II and yet we seem to have accomplished almost nothing, except lining the pockets of wartime profiteers and emptying our national treasury.

World War II colored American ideas about war as it should, but these conclusions are flawed by a lack of historical perspective. We all know that America never stood taller than in World War II. However, World War II was actually the second chapter of the Great War (WWI), and as such, it reflects a unique moment in world history. Drawing conclusions about the economics of war based upon such a unique moment in history leads to many misconceptions. These misconceptions about war make it easier to goad the American public to military action. Progressives can slow the militarization of America by refuting the tired and stale myths about war that make Americans less skeptical about going to war than they used to be.

Let us examine some of these powerful myths about war that Americans accept as proven facts. The myths born out of World War II have been leveraged to create further military dogma that seems accurate unless one takes the time to examine it.

War is good for the economy

This myth is based upon the fact that every one of the developed nations of the mid-twentieth century had their industrial infrastructure destroyed by war. Great Britain, Germany, Japan, China, and Russia/Soviet Union all had huge internal reconstruction to perform after the Second World War, after they had already struggled to recover from the First World War. American economic hegemony was assured after every potential competitor for #1 global economy was crippled by the Great War, chapter 2.0.

We then used our immense economic output to make sure, via the Marshall Plan and MacArthur's rebuilding in Japan, that we built future markets for our own goods. To guarantee this, we paid the markets to be reconstructed in our own image. We have reaped rewards for more than half a century from the economic circumstances that immediately followed WWII, but that unique situation cannot be used to drive our future economic decisions.

Germany rebuilt so quickly under Hitler that it feeds the myth that war is good for a nation's economy. Americans should reflect that certain economic indicators could look very positive when one does not pay workers a living wage or have to pay the workers at all. Huge profits can be made, but what of the dignity and freedom of the individual? We easily forget that economies operating on a wartime footing tend to be tied more closely to the state with no need to provide workers a living wage. This industrial-military connection creates an authoritarian capitalism that can boost economic output quickly. Businesses love the guaranteed profit margins from guaranteed military customers. To some, the rightful name of this corporate state is Fascist.

In the short term, wars can be good for economies if the aggressor nation loots and pillages everything it can from the nations it conquers. Germany tried to do that at the beginning of World War II, but could not hold what it had gained. The most basic failure of the neo-con agenda is it did not deliver the economic benefits that the control of the Iraq oil fields should have brought. Whether that failure was due to incompetence, corruption or ideological flaws will be debated for decades.

Even with such confiscatory war, it can be difficult for the aggressor nation to invest in its own infrastructure, as it has to spend so much time occupying, administrating, exploiting and holding the vanquished. The occupying nation must always expend resources to hold the occupied territories. Also, depending upon the persistence and resistance of the occupied, it can be a net negative even when a nation is confiscating all that is valuable from the conquered.

After a decade of war to start-off this century, our current economic circumstances should have finally put to bed the misconception that war is good for business. Unfortunately, military conflict is good for businesses that make profits off war machines, weapons and logistics. The military-industrial complex will keep pushing for more conflict no matter how bad it is for the overall economy in the long-term. This is one reason we currently make few investments in our own infrastructure or in our own people due to budget constraints caused by the costs of our foreign wars. We could find solace in the fact that it takes a long time for the bad consequences of poor infrastructure maintenance to be manifested, but we have been neglecting ours for too long. Now across America bridges are nearing collapse, our social safety net is being shredded and the education of our children has become third-rate, because war really IS NOT good for a nation's economy.

War drives innovations and great inventions.

Many believe that war drives invention and innovation. This is considered an unassailable fact in some quarters, but history does not really support this contention. War and the pressure to weaponize all technology often enhances great inventions, there is no question. Having acknowledged war can drive innovation, a surprising number of the great inventions that have changed the world over the last couple of centuries were not created by or for war. The list is long of the great peacetime inventions: the bicycle, automobile, telephone, radio, television, electric light, airplane, steam ships and locomotives are peacetime inventions all. These are undeniable peacetime inventions. Inventions created because of the peacetime information sharing that promotes huge leaps in creativity.

Some inventions seem to be undeniably weapons of war, but were really peacetime ideas. The rocket was "reinvented" by American Robert Goddard between the two world wars after the ancient Chinese technology had been lost. The computer came about in the 1930s, before World War II, though code breaking drove an incredible advancement of it during that war. Even the basic ideas of how to use nuclear fission to create energy were there before WWII drove us to weaponize it as the first atomic bomb. There is no denying that war can drive the refinement of existing technologies, but history seems to indicate that the great leaps of technology come from the synergies created through peace, not war.

There is a simple reason for the creativity found in peacetime and lack of it during wartime and that is national security interests. Wartime tends to lock up knowledge, not distribute it freely. Secrecy causes a loss of innovation. We can consider Chinese history for confirmation. A thousand years ago, China was a country with huge technological leads on rest of the world, gunpowder, rockets, and bombs were in the Chinese arsenal. Somehow, though, this technological lead all but disappeared by the time of the Opium Wars in the 19th century.

The mainstream history of China that Westerners heard for so long would have us believe that these technological advantages just were not weaponized. Now, more recent knowledge of Chinese history indicates that these technologies were weaponized. The Chinese did not just build fireworks; they built bombs and other explosive missiles. The Chinese enjoyed a technological advantage. They created weapons, which they deployed against their enemies. These weapons existed at the time of Marco Polo, but these were likely hidden from a foreigner.

Despite the national security interests of China, the secrets of gunpowder made it to Europe or Europeans invented it independently—although the latter seems doubtful. Europe was a chaotic political battleground and ideas on how to weaponize gunpowder spread quickly and widely. The lack of effective secrecy and nationalist conflicts on the European continent allowed for far more rapid development of gunpowder weaponry. The Chinese held a technological lead. The secrets of this technological lead became national security secrets to preserve a military advantage. Unfortunately, over time this secrecy eroded the Chinese technological lead and therefore their military advantage in the long term.

Since WWII, the US government has largely controlled innovation, creating a very similar dynamic. It is harder to find late 20th century examples of peacetime inventions. One world changing invention that does come to mind is the Internet, even though it started out as a DARPA military project. The Internet has empowered the people and become a source of further great innovation, in spite of the government and military's desires to keep the secrets locked away. The Internet is special, though. It was invented in the sixties and enhanced in the growing peacetime of the seventies. Invented in this special time in America, it can be seen as an exception due to the rebellious spirit of the time driving innovation, and despite military desires for secrecy. The Internet blossomed as a public entity, because the inventors refused to cooperate with the military-industrial complex. Such rebellion could not occur today, because the freedom of the individual has been greatly curtailed since the mid-20th century.

Secrecy limits the sharing of information, and without a collaborative knowledgebase, the synergies that accelerate development and invention simply cannot happen. In the case of China, it took hundreds of years before the European innovation machine surpassed the Chinese, but it did indeed eclipse Chinese technological advantages by the late 18th century and early 19th century. Currently, the pace of change is far greater and advantage will be lost much faster today.

The national security constraints of a constant wartime footing stifle innovation. In this environment, spying becomes the main path toward innovation, but it can only be exploited by the already established and financially well off. War justifies all manner of liberty rollbacks, but the espionage society prevents us from being the birthplace of the next great idea. The unconstitutional spying being done in this country is not being done to protect us, but instead, helps the moneyed and powerful to protect their interests. Under the guise of security, individual liberty is eroded by those with the money and power to exploit the lack of privacy in the surveillance society.

The CIA freely admits corporate moonlighting by agents today and few consider the negative implications for innovation in our country from this spy network. Surely, powerful, corporate interests will not pay for just anything. Powerful corporations will pay a high price, but only for high quality results. With CIA agents having access to all kinds of backdoors to privacy, they make perfect corporate spies. If the agent delivers, they can likely boost their bank account balance significantly. The Murdoch phone hacking scandals illustrate how intelligence can be used to boost corporate revenue.

War is bad for America, and it surely stifles growth and innovation.

War needn't be declared.

Since World War II America has spent trillions of dollars on foreign wars AND NONE of these wars have been declared. The executive branch of government must have some latitude to deploy troops for quick response in this dangerous world. Nonetheless, the legislative branch is where wars should be given the official backing of the people. Short-term troop deployments are one thing, but multi-year foreign occupations and invasions must be supported by a declaration of war. The military-industrial complex understands a formal declaration of war can be very difficult to achieve, better to have these slowly growing conflicts that eventually become full blown long term wars without having to face the full force of public debate in the beginning.

The legislative branch has shown itself to be somewhat spineless on the issue of war declarations and has repeatedly allowed executive branch troop deployments to drag on without any formal declaration of war. Legislative cowardice allowed Korea, Vietnam, Desert Storm, Afghanistan and Iraq to be prosecuted with no formal declaration of war. In the case of the latter three, the legislative branch passed bills abrogating them of their constitutional obligations.

This is where "the People" should step in and demand a formal declaration of war, preventing the legislature from turning its back on wartime responsibilities. Congress has proven they lack the political will without pressure from the people to debate a formal declaration of war no matter the consequences of their avoidance. Despite the many thousands of casualties in Korea, Vietnam, Afghanistan, and Iraq since World War II, Congress has not debated a war declaration resolution in 70 years!

The military draft is an evil scheme of the military-industrial complex.

Interestingly, a military draft need not be as completely evil as many claim. In fact, the Germans consider the military draft an absolute necessity to prevent the rise of another group like the Nazis. The National Socialist Party aligned itself with military interests and over time, the all-volunteer German army was populated with a large number of National Socialists. When Hitler came to power, the military supported his repeal of freedom and liberty, because they were all members of the same political party, the national Socialists or Nazis.

Americans now seem to be faced with an increasingly conservative, Christian and Republican military. This is almost completely a result of the all-volunteer army. America's republic is directly threatened by a combination of the military-industrial complex's lobbying for war and a political party that has aligned itself with the Pentagon and the defense industry. Without a draft, which brings into the military a broad cross section of society, the all-volunteer army tends to bring together a narrow segment of our society increasing the chances for dangerous groupthink.

Americans should consider a compulsory national service from our young people. One year of compulsory national service before the age of 26 need not be that onerous. They need not necessarily join an active branch of military, but there should be a very similar basic training program as part of the entry into a national service initiative. The individual could put in a full year by doing a summer in national service each summer of their college career. Entrants could choose whether they would enter a program like the Conservation Corp, a domestic Peace Corp, the National Guard, a military reservist role or an active duty military role.

Such a national service program makes the declaration of war more important, when so much of our youth might be on the line due to the national service program. Those that choose an active military role would be just that active duty military for at least a two-year hitch with the second year being worth a two-year scholarship to college. Each subsequent year of active duty would fund 1 further year of college tuition up to 8 years. Those that choose a reservist role or National Guard could only be called up to active military duty if a formal declaration of war is made in Congress. Those that choose a domestic Peace or Conservation Corp could opt out of active military service were war declared.

Having a national service program for our youth ensures that all segments of society have had some military or military-like training. This actually helps demilitarize the nation, because more and more civilians have had military training and can no longer be shouted down by a rabid and loud military special interest group as unpatriotic naïve civilians. Additionally, we would diminish the chance that our military becomes affiliated with just one political party, which is a tremendously dangerous situation.

We can always call on the "super powers" of the American military.

The current, strong and close Republican alliance with the military-industrial complex allows wartime profiteers to silently steer American foreign policy in directions that are not in the best interest of this nation. Consequently, Americans now have to accept the fact we will no longer be able to draw upon our historic military super powers. We must get used to being a nation that has peers.

The actions of the last decade have ended our status as the sole superpower and though this progressive agenda can help return America to greatness, we are not likely to regain the sole superpower status. We squandered that position in the first decade of this century. We may be able to hold our position as a first among equals and stabilize our finances, but it will be difficult to regain the historic super powers, unlimited money, and the unsurpassed technological leadership we once possessed. The world has changed too much. We can only work on ourselves and cannot control global evolution.

From the world's point of view, if we were still a superpower, we would have successfully prosecuted the wars in Afghanistan and Iraq. One of the nastiest consequences of the pre-emptive wars that America launched at the beginning of the 21st century is the loss of our superpower status. In the 1990s, we were perceived as the lone superpower. The world appeared to be in the beginnings of a Pax Americana, but that all began to unravel with our pre-emptive strike on Baghdad.

Now almost a decade later, the American superpower has been shown to have feet of clay. Not only have we lost the moral high ground that WWII had put us on, but also financially, we have been seriously weakened in the last few years. We live in a dangerous multi-polar world, which has yet to solidify into stable power blocs. America must recognize that we are no longer living in the bi-polar world of the Cold War or the unilateral American world that existed after the fall of the Soviet Union. We have in fact returned to the extremely dangerous and complicated multi-polar world that preceded the First Great World War.

As long as the United States is pinned down in foreign occupations, we are vulnerable to different military incursions against our interests worldwide. Even if we were to be able to unwind our foreign occupations, so that we could discourage such incursions, neither the Chinese nor the Russians really fear us any longer. Though neither nation can stand toe to toe with us in any given conflict, it is now clear that we do not have the financial wherewithal to sustain any long confrontation or deployment. Iraq and Afghanistan have sapped our military and financial resources, while boosting the profits of the military-industrial complex.

The invasions of Afghanistan and Iraq were necessary.

Afghanistan has long been nicknamed the graveyard of empires. Given the Soviet experience in the 1980s, no one would ever have dreamed that we would even consider such an invasion and occupation as we did in 2001. At the time, there was a bloodlust in the air, and Americans were demanding that the 9/11 attacks be avenged. However, to attack an entire nation for the acts of private individuals operating outside the bounds of national sovereignty seemed cruel, especially in light of the historical suffering of the Afghan people. In retrospect, it all seems a waste when our final solution for bin Laden involved a small strike team, not tens of thousands of boots on the ground. We fooled ourselves into believing that we were liberators of the Afghan people from the tyranny of the Taliban. In all likelihood, we will end up withdrawing after negotiating some kind of peace with the Taliban.

Iraq was another act that in retrospect makes no strategic sense, but does make economic sense for the military-industrial complex. We had already subjugated Iraq. The Kurds operated in an autonomous region, protected by the northern no-fly zone. In the South, the Shiites were similarly protected by a no-fly zone, and Saddam Hussein was effectively defanged. Of course, he was still making money off oil and perpetrating acts of terror on the ground within his own borders, but his ability to project his power was seriously curtailed. Additionally, Al-Qaeda was a Shiite organization, and Iraq was a Sunni-controlled nation. Given the rivalry between these two Muslim sects, almost all experts on the matter concluded that there was zero chance that Iraq and Al-Qaeda had joined forces or would do so in the future. Nonetheless, we went in and through the chaos we created, essentially set up Al-Qaeda in Iraq.

Now our coffers are empty. We may withdraw, claim some kind of victory, and call Iraq a single nation, but the Kurds are all but independent now. The Shiites and the Sunnis will never be able to form a government together and are likely to end up in separate autonomous regions as well. Iraq will continue to be a source of chaos and terrorism for generations to come, especially since the Shiite majority is easily manipulated by Iran, a Shiite nation.

These undeclared wars have lined the pockets of the military-industrial complex, but have done little to move forward any coherent American agenda or goals. The wars have been fought with little budgetary oversight and essentially been financed by Chinese bond purchases. Any confrontations with China from now until we pay this Chinese debt will always be colored by our status as a beggar nation. We must extricate ourselves from this mess, but it will take a long time.

We may have to consider scaling back our military commitments to allow us to pay some of this debt. Additionally, we should consider that scaling back our foreign occupations might not be what the Chinese want us to do. The Chinese have their own Muslim terrorist issues, and by funding the American occupations of Afghanistan and Iraq, the Chinese have the U.S. to act as a lightning rod for Muslim acts of terror.

The military-industrial complex is not a patriotic group. They are a for profit group with an eye to their bottom line. The fact that the money driving profits for the military-industrial complex is coming from Beijing does not cost their accountants any sleep. Ignoring corporate profits, we must accept that our invasion of these nations may have played right into the hands of the Chinese government.

Dogging the Dogma

The conservative backlash that swept Reagan into office brought with it a competing political narrative to the one that had dominated since the Depression and World War II. That earlier narrative had been one of equality, egalitarianism and social justice based upon the perceived mismanagement of the nation's economy by the moneyed and powerful leading to the Great Depression. The nation was looking down another tough road when Reagan came on the stage. The script he read from directly attacked certain ideas that had once been firmly entrenched in the minds of many Americans up until that time, namely that government could and should help the poor and the middle class.

The Republican right's resurgence in the latter half of the 20th century was largely based on game-changing views that had validity at the time, but now the time for those ideas is past too. Yet these narratives have become unassailable dogma in the 21st century despite how much the world has changed since the Reagan Revolution. Let us examine some of these myths from the eighties.

Unions are to blame for all manner of economic ills.

The reality is that less than 1 in 10 workers is a member of a union. Even the complete elimination of unions from the American social landscape could only have a limited effect on the economy. Unions have been in decline ever since the 1970s. Perhaps the opinion that the lack of American global competitiveness was due to greedy unions had some validity in the 1970s and 1980s when applied to the American automobile industry. The saying, as goes GM, so goes the country was a central tenet in the American economic vision and GM did not do well in the 1970s. The car industry had been a jewel in the American industrial crown and so when this industry so rapidly and dramatically failed it was a shock to the American psyche. The blame game began and unions were the scapegoats.

In the 1970s with the oil embargos, the American auto industry fell on hard times. Some of the decline could be blamed on the shoddy workmanship coming out of the Detroit factories, but not all of it.

The American auto industry did not control geopolitics of the day and that had something to do with the auto industry's downturn going into the 1980s. Corporate America wants nothing more than the complete elimination of unions, because corporations are moneymaking enterprises. The forty-hour workweek, paid overtime, holidays and health benefits are all drags upon the bottom line. These most basic expectations of an employee from a job were all hard-fought battles won for the American worker by unions in the Great Depression and before.

Cutting taxes always leads to greater tax revenue.

The Laffer curve was not proven by any economic numbers in the Reagan Renaissance. As detailed elsewhere, the Reagan era changes to the tax code targeted the middle class heavily with the huge Social Security tax increase. Government spending went up and tax revenue sources shifted significantly away from corporations and high-income earners that is true, but that hardly demonstrates any lightening of the tax burden directly raising revenues. The 1980s saw a shifting of the burden from the powerful to the less powerful, not a true tax cut for everyone.

The turnaround of the American economy in the mid eighties and strong surge of the 1990s was based upon deficit spending. Government spending is an economic stimulant and when the government keeps looting the huge Social Security Trust Fund to pay for its budget deficits the economy grows. It is arguable that giving tax breaks to corporations is the most effective way to provide the greatest economic benefit for the greatest number. In fact, given the giant pile of debt and our economic frailty there is plenty of evidence that it is not.

Any lingering doubts about cutting taxes creating jobs should be put to bed by the enormous Bush tax cuts that did not create many jobs. The reality is that job growth was the most anemic for any president on record after these tax cuts were instituted. These tax cuts did nothing but create the spectacular deficits we now face. An enormous amount of money is being squandered on foreign occupations and military adventures. Funding these military occupations has added significantly to the national debt and the off budget costs of these wars require an increase in revenue. Always cutting taxes, especially for the rich and corporate does not seem to have yielded the economic miracle that twenty plus years of such medicine ought to have brought about...were it true.

The Mainstream Media is biased toward the liberal point of view.

Media today is diverse and driven by the <u>pull</u> model, where the consumer pulls the content he wants and ignores that which he does not. This means that Americans no longer hear points of view they might disagree with. In the old media model, it was <u>push</u> where a limited number of networks, news shows and big name journalists pushed their content out. This meant journalists with TV time had great power. This liberal bias myth seems to have gotten its start in the time of the push model and with Walter Cronkite famously turning against the Vietnam War.

Today the mainstream media's cheerleading of the Iraq invasion and occupation during the run-up to that disastrous conflict demonstrates the entertainment nature of news today. Today journalists need to be <u>pulled</u> in by the consumer rather than get <u>pushed</u> out to a captive audience. In the run up to the preemptive war against Iraq, the only bias shown was the bias to parrot the propaganda being spoon fed to the media outlets at the time by the government and military.

Nonetheless, the liberal bias myth persists. Many liberal ideas came to full flower during the sixties and seventies. Events of the time also turned journalists into celebrities, such as Woodward and Bernstein. Their famous destruction of the Nixon presidency forever put journalists in the cross hairs of conservative Republicans. Watergate is often used to prove the liberal bias even though it was forty years ago.

Watergate may seem to indicate that there "was" perhaps a liberal bias, but that is about it. Still, current analysis of the Watergate affair would seem to indicate a shadowy power struggle between the FBI and the CIA. The Washington Post appears to simply have been a convenient tool of the FBI leaker, Deep Throat.

To many, Watergate appeared to represent a case of conservatives being skewered by a biased newspaper, but a more accurate interpretation indicates a dangerous lack of transparency in government. Now that ex-CIA agent Bob Woodward has fingered ex-Deputy FBI director Marc Felt as Deep Throat, a thinking person feels there is more to this story than Woodward is revealing. For one, it is convenient that Marc Felt is no longer capable of denying or confirming his role as Deep Throat. Secondly, Deep Throat clearly warns Woodward that their lives are in danger as the Watergate scandal unfolds.

Watergate does not confirm the liberal bias in media, but rather confirms that the mainstream media has failed utterly in its task as an independent voice that asks the tough questions in American society. Tough questions, such as who in American government then had the power to threaten the life of the Deputy Director of the FBI? And who wields that power today?

Privatize everything because government fails at everything.

Americans are quite schizophrenic in their relationship with their government. They will loudly complain about government incompetence, but fully expect Social Security and Medicare to keep sending those checks. We drive on an impressive interstate highway system conceived, financed and executed by our government. These are clear signs that government can do things that are positive.

Privatization only has its place when it does not create a monopoly. For example, California's deregulation of electricity was disastrous. Greedy outsiders played the market and drove up prices fleecing the state for billions. Consumers had only one wire coming to their houses. There was no real competition other than going down to the hardware store and getting a large diesel generator. Enron and other Texas power brokers manipulated electrical generation to rip-off billions from California electrical consumers.

Government has fixed some things in our society, we must admit. Medicare was created, because private insurers refused to insure older people, because they were more likely to get sick. The central government's design and financing of our national highway system has made trillions for American business. There are things that big government can do well.

Regulating our banking and financial system was a huge role that the government was thrust into during the Great Depression, but has gradually scaled back to almost nothing. The reduction of regulation and controls on our financial system had catastrophic consequences, which are still being felt today. Proper government regulation would have prevented the horrors of the 2008 financial crisis.

Today there are opportunities for government to help and empower citizens. Just as the highway system has been invaluable to business, the information highway called the Internet could be improved by government intervention. Municipalities have tried to get into the Internet provider business, because the private sector projects were too expensive. Cities had some infrastructure they could leverage to create wireless broadband points across their jurisdictions. Corporations have lobbied hard to prevent municipalities from providing wireless internet services.

Private corporations do not operate in the public good. They are selfish institutions. Recognizing that public utilities have a place in our society will be the first step toward allowing public Wi-Fi to enrich our nation. These public Wi-Fi implementations can also serve to broaden a new American Commons.

The Space Program is a waste of money.

The American space program has been pared down to the bare bones and is a mere shadow of its former self. The program that put the first human on another planet is starved for funding. With all our budgetary problems, it is easy to cut the space program. The dividends from investing in space technologies are highly speculative and hard to predict. Those technological leaps that pursuing a space program provides have national security implications, though. Economic efficiencies can come from space-related inventions and often space technologies can be rather easily weaponized as well.

America should not cede a moon base to China! Frozen water has been verified in moon craters in very large quantities. Quantities that provide a moon base with all the raw materials for maintaining an independent existence. Water has its obvious uses, but it can also be split at the molecular level to provide fuel, hydrogen, and atmosphere, oxygen, for the base. A base could be engaged in mining operations, most likely, but many other high tech projects as well.

With so much of America's military budget geared to supply large foreign occupations, we lack the innovations that would occur in a healthy research and development budget of a rich nation. We lack the funding to push research and development projects, like the U.S. space program of the sixties. Ending foreign occupation could immediately fund a new push to colonize beyond Earth. We cannot afford to have the Chinese and Russians fund their space programs so effectively, while we simply retire our shuttles and ask the private sector to pick up the slack.

Not to mention, there are military advantages to investing in our space program. We must invest some big money here due to future intangible technological advantage. Doubters need only read Robert Heinlein's <u>The Moon is a Harsh Mistress.</u>

Affirmative Action in America

The race issue in America is rarely discussed honestly. It is such a volatile issue that few people can speak openly about exactly what they feel. The fact that we teach our children that the Civil War was mostly about states' rights, because the slavery issue is such an emotional one, is illustrative of this. Slavery was so truly horrible that most Americans want to avoid it, denying it was the true cause of the conflict. When the races mix in America, the racial tensions are still there, unarticulated and yet we are more diverse than ever. Everyone keeps their true feelings and thoughts to themselves for fear of offending others. We cannot continue like this as a nation.

Racial tensions are still very real in America, but the symptoms are underground and encoded. Progress is difficult on other issues as long as we cannot really heal this wound as a nation. Only open and frank discussion of race in America can bring that healing. Obama's election to the highest office in the land most certainly indicates progress, but the fanatical opposition also indicates a need to open up about race in America. Race relations have deteriorated recently despite Obama's election to the White House. The Tea Party and the Birthers are a symptom of these continuing racial tensions. The creation of these political groups did not occur in a vacuum. The commentary of alleged experts in these matters leaves too much unsaid.

Yes, we have progressed, but much of that progress was compelled by law and not always through social evolution. Race distorts our opinions, our politics and clouds our vision. The first presidential administration of this century was so disastrous that the country was desperate for change, hence Barack Obama's presidency. This is certainly a commendable outcome as it relates to race anyway. Nonetheless, Obama's election was not unanimous. Portions of the extreme right wing are obviously driven by an indignation over a Kenyan-American as President. They feverishly search for proof of a non-Hawaiian birth certificate. The birth certificate issue seems driven by desperate opposition to a black man as president. Common sense indicates that there would be no way that both the Democrats AND the Republicans would ever have let Obama get all the way to the White House without vetting his citizenship completely. The Republicans could have won the presidency could they have proven him a non-citizen and there is no way Democrats would have wanted to put up a candidate with a skeleton like that in their closet.

Racial tensions partially drove opposition and jealousy to public sector unions in Wisconsin and other states. These anti-public sector union feelings can be traced to some of this intractable racism. It matters that affirmative action has been getting people of color into public sector jobs. These jobs were coveted and affirmative action severely curtailed the ability for white male citizens to get these jobs for over 40 years. The Republicans in Wisconsin were able to tap into this envy of public sector workers to push through a draconian reduction in the public sector unions' collective bargaining abilities.

Affirmative action exacerbates the problem of racial tension on the street. Government tinkering in the job market has forced extreme color sensitivity into every corner of the economy. This sensitivity has increased as the job market has become tighter and tighter. Promoting color blindness on the street should be our objective. In today's high unemployment environment, affirmative action forces race into the intense competition for jobs.

Many that actually benefit feel that affirmative action is demeaning. There are always the whispered accusations that they could not have made it without the program. These people know, in fact, that they made it based on their own hard work, not affirmative action, and they resent the stigma. They want to remove this stigma attached to their achievements.

That does not mean that we should not attempt to make reparations for past sins. There are still those that feel disenfranchised, and they attribute this to years of racism. Slavery was such a horrific institution it is hard to debate that 150 years after the end of slavery that there is not still damage to the descendants. The only way we can put the consequences of slavery and racism behind us is to address these concerns. A new focus for affirmative action can be a lightning rod to attract a positive healing energy. Affirmative action, when applied to representative government, has more validity. Seeding into the legislature a percentage of a specific racial or cultural group could make sense.

America can pay this social and cultural reparation. Instead of micro managing the business world, affirmative action can be applied to representative democracy. In this way, we can macroscopically affect American society. Permanently sharing power with the two minorities most oppressed over the last two centuries is a real world compromise and not a bribe. The government's experiment to tip the playing field of business in favor of one race or another should be curtailed.

We need a narrowing of the focus of affirmative action as well. It does not make sense that the current version of affirmative action applies to well over 50% of the population. In fact, at best, white males make up about 30% of the new diverse America, and for the most part, this is the only portion of society not covered by affirmative action. A ratio like that makes the program appear to be a tyranny of the majority over the minority. A new version of affirmative action should only be applied to the two minorities most discriminated against in our history.

Make no mistake Black America has suffered mightily under the American flag. Black-America is beginning to realize its political power, though. Barack Obama has certainly changed the conversation. Still there seems to be a need to pay some reparation to make up for the slavery and racism. Additionally, having the predominantly black Washington, D.C. represented by a "Shadow Senator" in the Senate seems a bit racist. The District of Columbia could serve as a vehicle for Black-American statehood. This new state's political boundaries will extend beyond the current limits. As an enduring reparation, instead of the current version of affirmative action, America will give Black-America statehood.

All who consider themselves "black" will have the option to vote in this abstract state. Two senators will be for D.C. itself, and another two will be for those living outside the district, based upon registration rolls.

We should assign as many representatives as their voter registration indicates. It would be ironic if the name of Columbus came to be attached with ideas of political inclusion in the District of Columbia. People of color have so long reviled foolish, cruel and greedy Chris.

Arguably, Native Americans have suffered the most at the hands of the American government. Affirmative action has helped them the least. As a people, they have all but disappeared. As a percentage of the population, they are less than 1%. For decades, the Native Americans lived on the fringes of our society in semi-autonomous regions called reservations. Only in the last few years have these autonomous regions become lucrative gambling meccas. The reservations should be admitted to the US as a state to guarantee their voice as part of the legislature.

Reservations are America's answer to the homelands of the old South Africa. American Indians, Eskimos, and Hawaiians have traditionally received the short end of the stick in our society. Currently, the indigenous peoples appear to have gotten their revenge as they pocket millions, taking advantage of the white man's gambling obsessions. Nonetheless, the scarcity of full-blooded Native Americans is a true tragedy.

The five largest remaining American Indian tribes, the Cherokee, the Navajo, the Chippewa, the Sioux, and the Choctaw, could get two seats each in the House of Representatives. Those five tribes represent less than a million souls. The Eskimos and the Hawaiians should also receive two seats each. The remaining native peoples should get an additional four seats. They should be newly created seats, not taken from the current pool. Also, the entire population of native peoples, Eskimos and Hawaiians, should be admitted as a state and be given two senators.

We should enfranchise these people. The indigenous people have already economically seceded. They supply their own entire infrastructure in many places. America needs native energy going into our future. We should hope they would accept statehood as the olive branch it is meant to be.

Women are another major group with a stake in affirmative action. However, the high unemployment rates among men in the Great Recession demonstrate the growing economic power of women in the 21st century. Admittedly, women still have not penetrated the old boy's network of national politics to the degree one would expect, given their percentage of society. Women make up over one-half of the electorate, yet they represent a far smaller percentage of the Senate and House of Representatives.

Undoubtedly, women are woefully under-represented. However, a case can be made that the blame for this falls at the feet of women themselves. Women have not exercised their obvious electoral power. Women are not really a minority. They are an apathetic majority. Women make up more than 50% of voters. They need only to exercise the power that they already have. Getting a woman in the Oval Office should be a breeze!

Hispanics are also a significant factor in the affirmative action debate. However, Latin America is not waiting for the United States to share power. They are demographically absorbing California and the rest of the Border States that were seized during the American Invasion of Mexico in 1840. The solutions to illegal immigration will have far-reaching diplomatic implications as well as social ones. Affirmative action does little to deal with these other facets of the Hispanic question.

Affirmative action was not solely about race when it was created, but also about economics. Racism had left certain segments of society poverty-stricken. This is much less so today. Poverty is affecting a very diverse ethnic and racial group. It makes sense to create an economic affirmative action at colleges and other appropriate institutions for the economically handicapped. We cannot continue to pit the races against each other in college and in the job market when there are so many unemployed.

No question DC statehood as a reparation for slavery faces many practical obstacles. The idea of broader virtual boundaries for the District of Columbia would be even more controversial and criticized for its impracticality. Nonetheless, acknowledging our continuing racial tensions is a prerequisite for healing our nation's racial wounds and considering the aforementioned could go a long way in that direction. We can replace the current un-American affirmative action plan with these 21st century alternatives and move our country forward.

Final Thoughts

Progressives Should Support a Flag Burning Amendment

Politicians love to wrap themselves in the flag. They cannot resist the loyalty and power that hyper-patriotic nationalism bestows upon them. The Republicans did a very good job of leveraging this aspect of mass manipulation after 9/11. To question Republican initiatives was to be labeled unpatriotic, and Democrats ran for cover after 09/11/2001. In the same vein, progressives should see what an opportunity a Flag Desecration amendment could be to potentially tip the electoral scales in their favor. Progressives see an opening for political gain in a hyper-patriotic push for a flag desecration amendment.

Here is a plan to boost progressive electoral power. Progressives should put forward an amendment on flag desecration. In the meantime, while the amendment makes its way through the state houses, progressives should attempt to push through a federal law defining violations of the Flag Code as felonies. Right-wing Republicans will be enthusiastic for this, but they could rue the day. In such an amendment, progressives will have set a trap to limit opposition to the progressive libertarian-socialist agenda.

Stars-and-Stripes swag is de rigueur for today's right-wing conservative. On everything from ties, hats, and even bug deflectors, right-wingers feel naked unless they can wrap themselves in the flag. Conservatives will not see the potential for problems when progressives begin to pursue the old right-wing course of prosecuting flag desecration. Few will remember persecuting hippies for displaying the flag everywhere during the sixties. An American flag patch on the bottom of one's ratty jeans or a stylized flag on one's motorcycle helmet or other such "protest" displays could get one beat up, back in the day anyway.

Nowadays, it is the conservatives displaying the flag in all these forms, not the pinko longhairs.

The term "desecration" does have some ambiguity to it and this can be used to progressive advantage. Is desecration burning the flag? No, it cannot be that, because the proper disposal of a flag that is no longer in serviceable condition is for it to be burned. To properly prosecute the perpetrator of a flag burning, said perpetrator would almost have to admit that the burning was an act of desecration. Otherwise, the burner could simply state that the flag was no longer in respectable condition. We would need to have thought police to determine the true intent of a flag burning, if the burner were to plead flag code adherence as an excuse. Progressives will need a more useful definition of desecration to take full advantage.

In an effort to narrowly define desecration, progressives should inject specifics of the flag code into the law to remove ambiguity. Failure to adhere to the flag code will be, by definition, desecration. To remove ambiguity, progressives will force in language more exactly defining the current flag code as well as increasing the penalties for desecration to something quite onerous—for example, make it a felony, punishable by at least 5 years in jail. Progressives can get clarifications inserted in the flag code to leverage the amendment for its maximum political impact.

Progressives will define exactly the criteria for making a flag unserviceable and, therefore making continued use, desecration and mandating its disposal. In this digital imaging age, it will be quite easy to distribute small cards with the approved shades of red, white, and blue. That way, it will be easy to see when a flag needs to be retired by simply comparing the colors on a candidate flag that may have faded beyond acceptable limits to the government approved "These Colors Don't Run" flag desecration, color match card. The flag code could also be enhanced to state exactly how many foot-candles of light must be falling on an American flag that is displayed at night. In addition, the definition of rain should include exactly how many drops per square inch defines "rain" as well as similar benchmarks for other types of precipitation. All-weather flags will be specifically defined to narrow the ability of displayers to claim their flag is all weather. Any weather that could potentially damage the flag will be enumerated, but the verbiage from the flag code is vague and allows for flexible enforcement.

A flag desecration amendment presents a tremendous opportunity to remove the super (pseudo) patriots who will stand in the way of a progressive movement and who fly the American flag 24/7 in front of their houses and on their automobiles. The aforementioned verbiage clarifications will set the trap. These hyper-patriotic persons are almost exclusively of the political stripe that will oppose a progressive agenda vehemently. This legislative action will help reduce their numbers. Progressives know that the hyper-patriots regularly violate the flag code, based upon the fact that their hyper-patriotic nationalism compels them to fly the flag non-stop.

By flying the flag 24/7, the flag tends to become faded and tattered in short order. These alleged patriots never take the flag down, and this rapidly ages the Stars and Stripes. Similarly, during raining or inclement weather, they do not take the flag down as the flag code specifies, but let it fly in drenching rains. This further damages the flag and disrespects it. Also, by flying the flag of this nation 24/7, the hyper-patriots leave their flags up past sunset most of the time, if they take it in at all, ever. There will be numerous opportunities to get progressive opponents off the street and incarcerated for the heinous act of flag desecration.

The progressive line will be simple and direct. The ability to remove the flag desecraters from the streets of America will make things safer in America. After all, flag desecration is a serious offense and sets a very poor example for our youth. The flag code clearly states that the flag should be brought in after sunset unless a spotlight is shined directly upon it. A porch light 50 feet away in a doorway would not qualify. The flag code also clearly states the flag should be brought in during inclement weather. Also, with exact color definitions, RGB in our digital age, for the official colors of the American flag, those flags that are faded and ready for burning will be readily identifiable.

There is one more layer to the progressive guile of laying a trap for their extremist enemies. The widespread display of the Confederate flag by reactionary southerners will be a particular target for this flag desecration amendment. Everyone knows, of course, that the Confederate flag was the banner of secession and treason, as the Union saw it. But most people don't know that the Confederate flag design itself was a physical desecration of the Stars and Stripes. It was a deliberate taking of the physical elements of the Union flag to rearrange them in a parody. It was meant to anger the Union and symbolically split the flag as the South wanted to split the union.

All displays of this treasonous banner would have to cease, but this outcome would not be part of the initial activism to get the flag desecration laws passed. Instead, this would be an outcome that progressives would keep to themselves and apply later. Continued displays of the banner could be viewed as more than just desecration, but actual treasonous incitement of the masses. With many intolerant jingoistic southerners cooling their heels in Gitmo detention for flag desecration and potentially high treason, the progressives should have no trouble taking the South in the Electoral College.

Think of the growth of progressive power, as more and more pseudo-patriotic extremists are rightfully imprisoned for their desecration transgressions. The progressives might even be able to get large mandatory sentencing guidelines pushed through, along with the amendment to prevent activist judges that oppose the progressive agenda from trying to let their compatriots off with a wrist slap. This is how political power is seized in America. The Republicans have broken the necessary ground, demonstrating the efficacy of this methodology.

OK, ...stop, this flag desecration essay is pure theatre. Despite my immense respect for that Star-Spangled Banner, progressives cannot support an amendment against flag desecration. If you believed I was serious, sorry, just trying to make a point and to get your creative juices flowing. The preceding is to demonstrate how law and order pitches or hyper-patriotic law making can be used against political enemies and can very well change the make-up of the electorate. Caution must be exercised here and our passions restrained.

If you read the preceding and were gung-ho to execute the aforementioned plan against the opponents of progressives, then, please stop here and reread this book. Freedom is messy and tolerance a key necessity to success, due to the high emotions that fuel all political endeavor. In the real world unrestrained freedom and individual liberty can lead to mob rule rather than reasoned rule. The French Revolution is a cautionary tale in this respect. The ability of the electorate to be immune to manipulations of the aforementioned kind will be key to a successful reinvigoration of America.

The Bicycle Shall Lead the Way

Progressives will need to embrace the ideal that there are strong synergies created by individual freedom. An embrace it must be, because there is no question that individual freedom is a scary thing. People will have more freedom to be stupid as individual liberty increases under this progressive course. There is the actual likelihood that society will be less safe in some ways, though more safe in other more important ones. Freedom is not having to allow your wife or daughter strip-searched at the airport. Nonetheless, there is something very scary about allowing individuals to be free, because one's fellow citizens will have the freedom to make bad choices.

Life is full of risk, and our nation's return to greatness will travel a risky road, there is no doubt. We will be trusting in our fellow citizens to use their new freedoms wisely or at least not destructively. Trust is a difficult word for Americans these days, but trust our fellow Americans, we must. Sometimes, even I doubt my fellow Americans' sanity and responsibility, given the current state of affairs.

Despite my doubts about American sanity and responsibility, as a bicycle commuter, I put my life in the hands of my fellow Americans several times a week. Essentially, I trust that Republicans and Democrats et al will at least drive responsibly. I put faith in the system of licensing that trains and then tests drivers before allowing them to drive. This is a system of licensing that is run by government. The government is licensing citizens to command a deadly weapon on the road after some training and testing. There is a distinctive libertarian nature to bicycle commuting as I trust my fellow citizens to be responsible drivers with limited oversight by authorities.

Over the years, I have often commuted to my jobs on a bicycle. I found that I did not have the disposition for the gym and would rarely go. However, one must get to work and that generally involves a commute. Most of the time, I have found ways to commute on a bicycle at least some days, and it has paid off in health benefits for me over the years.

That is not to say that there are no risks to bicycle commuting. I have to ride in traffic and share the road with multi-ton vehicles that are operated by strangers of varying degrees of driving skill. After having commuted tens of thousands of miles, I have to thank the driving skills of many anonymous American drivers over the years to be able to write this. I have had to trust my fellow Americans with my life, and they have come through for me. That experience makes it easier for me to embrace the idea of freeing my fellow Americans so that they might lead this country back to greatness.

Not only has my bicycle commuting allowed me to trust my fellow Americans more, I have also realized what a powerful and efficient machine the bicycle is. I have saved many gallons of gasoline and doctor bills through the benefits of this wonderful machine, but it goes beyond these basic positives. The invention and widespread adoption of the bicycle in the late 19th century changed the world, but America especially. The bicycle is an incredibly efficient device when it comes to converting human effort into distance. The bicycle became a great equalizer for the poor, but hard-working soul in America. Previously, transportation independence required a horse and a horse required a lot of food, housing and other maintenance that was relatively costly. The bicycle brought to the common man a means of transportation that could simply be parked overnight without food or water being required.

The bicycle was a game changer as we entered the 20th century, becoming a platform for many early internal combustion engines. The rise of the automobile diminished the bicycle's importance in the West, but in much of the developing world, it continued to be the go to vehicle. A case could be made that China's current economic power had its germination in the efficient use of the bicycle by the populace for much of the 20th century.

During WWII, the Dutch utilized the bicycle to continue to resist the Germans. The Germans had stripped the country of mechanized vehicles. Those vehicles not confiscated were useless because all the fuel was under German control as well. The Dutch were left with their bicycles. The Dutch leveraged these human powered vehicles to create chaos and sabotage all across Holland. The two-wheeled partisans of the Netherlands were a pain in Hitler's @$$ the entire war.

Now in the 21st century, the bicycle provides an opportunity in our society where we can experiment with rolling back our legal Nanny-state. Right now, for all practical purposes in America, bicycles do not really have to follow traffic laws. Of course, on the books, they are supposed to follow the traffic laws, but in practical terms, the police mostly ignore the bicyclist. Police understand the dangerous and vulnerable position the cyclist is in. Unless a cyclist engages in extremely dangerous behavior, police allow bicyclists a certain amount of latitude as it relates to traffic law. Many cities ban cyclists on sidewalks, but on certain busy streets, riding on the sidewalk is the only sane thing to do. The police often blithely allow it as common sense policing by not enforcing a stupid and dangerous law.

In the bicycle, we have a machine that can help us conserve fuel and cut down on gridlock and pollution. Large-scale adoption of commuting by bicycle would bring untold benefits, many of them intangible and difficult to predict, but benefits will be delivered for sure. Instead of having the police give bicyclists an "unofficial" pass on traffic laws, we could institutionalize the freedom of the bicycle. Simply exempt bicyclists from all traffic laws nationally except where the cyclists endanger others.

By exempting cyclists from traffic law, we can take a step in this grand experiment to inject greater freedom into our society. Police would still be allowed to ticket or even arrest cycling citizens for truly reckless behavior. On the other hand, police will allow cyclists to choose whether they will come to a full stop at that stop sign or ride on the sidewalk. Put cyclists on their honor to not make mischief for the rest of society and allow them unprecedented freedom.

There are very positive social effects to be achieved by this cycling freedom experiment. This national policy will encourage a hardy breed of Americans that wish to be freer to adopt the bicycle as their main mode of transportation. Freedom of requirements to carry papers, like drivers licenses, or the freedom to ignore that stop sign, because you are a human powered vehicle should be powerful motivators for the true American. Non-riders who object will just have to accept that a good look both ways at a slow clip on a bike conserves enormous energy for the rider and allows them sufficient time to assess whether it is safe or not. Over long distances, this energy conservation is essential to actually completing one's commute sometimes.

Doubters of the great libertarian-socialist experiment that this book promotes can start their research on the wheels of a bicycle. It is so appropriate that this be the vehicle to demonstrate the validity of the ideas of freedom AND social interconnection. The bicycle is one of the most efficient machines ever invented to convert work into distance. The bicycle is an invention of peacetime that became the basis of a mechanical world, first for the individual unable to afford a horse and then as a platform for small engines ushering in the great petroleum-based modern world.

Many people currently in power see the average American as a lazy slug that will never change their ways and deserves abridgement of their rights due to their weak will. The bicycle holds the key to change some of the current calculus in America's balance of trade AND demonstrate the power of free individuals. If even a small percentage of Americans switched to bicycle commuting, the amount of energy and money saved would be enormous. If large numbers of Americans biked a couple thousand miles a year on their commutes, healthcare costs would likely fall and the energy savings could make America completely energy independent, especially if it is in conjunction with a strong nuclear power program.

Progressives on bicycles can truly alter the entire playing field. Progressives can be the true game changers. Two-wheeled progressives completely change the economic calculus that currently seems to doom America. Two-wheeled progressives in sufficient numbers can deliver a future that is unimagined by anyone right now. Citizens and politicians could wake up in ten years and see the country in the black again. The power of the people would be clearly and unequivocally demonstrated by such an economic and social miracle. Politicians would have to acknowledge the power of the people. The people would gain the confidence that freedom and individual liberty really is the right answer just as Ben Franklin had said at the very beginning!

All that has come before in this book is interconnected and the bicycle is no exception. We must deliver the economic miracle to ourselves, not to the moneyed and the powerful. We cannot deliver the miracle, if we are divided. The people will have to stop fighting over the scraps and work together to take back the economy and the country. These pages are meant to convince Americans that there are solutions to the seemingly insoluble issues before us and therefore a reason to come together.

Of course, the pages that came before certainly advocated spending some money. This is not an austerity program. The bicycle can seriously help fund the progressive agenda that has been outlined here, but not all of it. This agenda really is not pie in the sky. It is a plan to progressively restore American greatness based on common sense and hard work. What could be more patriotic than that?

Epilogue

This book pens out a libertarian-socialist agenda that could be called progressive—an agenda that outlines a new political vision a majority of Americans could support. Political writing these days seeks to divide rather than unite. We have been unable to move ahead as a country because of all that divides us.

Perhaps it has taken me too long to write this book, but I had to get it out there once I had something. I was not quite sure that I had a coherent plan that could work...until now. This is my attempt at defining a new middle ground for America where we can come together to help our country progress and evolve into a freer, more peaceful and more economically secure society.

Is this that new unifying vision? Only time will tell if it is.

DONT TREAD ON ME

Incidentally, while writing this book, I came up with my own little banner (see above) to fly on my bicycle while commuting. You can get a 2-Wheeled Progressive battle flag for your bicycle, read the Progressive Restoration blog and purchase copies of this book at www.TheProgressiveRestoration.com

###